NEW IRISH WALK GUIDES

East and South

David Herman & Miriam Joyce McCarthy

GENERAL EDITOR
JOSS LYNAM

Gill and Macmillan

Published in Ireland by
Gill and Macmillan Ltd
Goldenbridge
Dublin 8
with associated companies in
Auckland, Delhi, Gaborone, Hamburg, Harare,
Hong Kong, Johannesburg, Kuala Lumpur, Lagos, London,
Manzini, Melbourne, Mexico City, Nairobi,
New York, Singapore, Toyko
© David Herman and Miriam Joyce McCarthy, 1991
Maps by Nuala Creagh
0 7171 1794 4
Print origination by
Seton Music Graphics Ltd, Bantry, Co. Cork
Printed by
The Guernsey Press

Based on the Ordnance Survey
by permission of the Government
(Permit No. 5429)

CONTENTS

MOUNTAIN SAFETY

The Irish hills are still relatively unfrequented. This is a happy situation for hill walkers unless they get into serious trouble and need help. As this may well have to come from a considerable distance, it is particularly important to take all reasonable precautions.

1. Wear suitable clothing, and regardless of the weather carry extra warm clothes, wind- and water-proof anorak and overtrousers. Except on short, easy walks it is best to wear walking boots.

2. Plan your walk carefully and be sure you can complete it before dark. To estimate walking times see page 3.

3. Check weather forecasts and keep a look out for weather changes. On high ground mist and rain can close in with alarming speed.

4. Remember that the temperature drops 2–3°C for each 300m/1,000ft you climb and if, as is frequently the case, there is a strong wind the temperature drop will be even more marked. It may be a pleasant day at sea level whilst freezing and windy at 800m/2,500ft.

5. Always carry a map and compass, and learn to use them efficiently in good weather so you will have confidence in your ability to use them in bad. A torch, whistle and small first aid kit should also be taken — remember that the mountain distress signal is six blasts per minute and then a pause.

6. Carry a reserve supply of food including chocolate, glucose tablets, etc., and something warm to drink.

7. Leave word at your hotel, guest house or hostel where you are going, what your route will be and when you intend to get back. If you are parking a car at the beginning of a walk, you can leave a note on the seat.

8. Streams in flood are dangerous and extreme caution is necessary.

9. If your party does have an accident, telephone 999 and ask for the Mountain Rescue or contact the local Garda Station who will organise the rescue.

10. Never walk solo, except in areas where there are other people around.

11. Remember that most accidents happen on the descent, when you are tired, so take especial care then.

Some of the precautions listed above are obviously designed for the longer, higher walks but do remember that especially in winter, the Irish hills can be dangerous.

The Country Code
- GUARD AGAINST FIRE. Every year carelessness costs thousands of pounds.
- FASTEN ALL GATES. Animals will wander if they can.
- KEEP DOGS UNDER CONTROL. They should be on a lead wherever there is livestock.

- KEEP TO PATHS ACROSS FARMLAND.
- AVOID DAMAGING FENCES, HEDGES AND WALLS.
- LEAVE NO LITTER.
- SAFEGUARD WATER SUPPLIES. Do not pollute streams, ponds or water troughs.
- PROTECT WILDLIFE, PLANTS AND TREES.
- GO CAREFULLY ON COUNTRY ROADS. Single file, facing oncoming traffic.
- RESPECT THE LIFE OF THE COUNTRYSIDE.

MAPS AND SCALES

The Republic of Ireland is in the process of a complete re-survey and re-issue of its small-scale maps, changing from imperial to metric units. This has created some problems for us in that the re-survey has shown up some minor errors in heights, so that the new metric height is often not a simple conversion from the old height in feet. Where there are old maps in print as well as new ones, we have given in the text the two heights as shown on the maps, even where these are not exactly compatible; where we have only one height, be it metric or imperial, we have made a strict conversion. In a year or two this may pose a few problems for readers, in that new metric maps will have metric heights which may differ from the converted heights we have listed. This small problem is more than compensated by the better quality of the new 1:50,000 maps as compared with the old ½ inch ones.

Where heights or distances are approximate, as in 'walk 300yds along the road and turn off at a stile,' we have not been pedantic and converted this to '274.3m,' but, since the instruction is clearly to give an approximate distance, have simply written '270m/300yds'.

While the sketch maps in this book will give you a good idea of your route, they are hardly sufficient, especially on the more mountainous walks, as complete guides, and you are strongly advised to use the relevant topographical map. The maps available in the spring of 1991 are as follows:

Ordnance Survey maps:
1:250,000 Holiday map. Sheet 3
(This is suitable for general planning.)
Half-inch to 1 mile (1:126,720) maps. Sheets 16, 18, 19, and 22
(These are out-of-date, and really too small for walkers, but in many areas they are the only maps available.)
1 inch to 1 mile (1:63,360) map. Sheet Wicklow District
(Beware! The contour interval changes from 100ft (30m) below 1,000ft (300m) to 250ft (75m) above 1,000ft.)
1:50,000 (1¼ ins to 1 mile) map. Sheets 54, 56, and Wicklow Way
(These maps are up-to-date, and of good quality; further sheets are being issued, so you should enquire if any more are available.)

Walking Times

Walking times have been calculated on the basis of 4km per hour, and 400m ascent per hour. This is roughly equivalent to 2½ miles per hour, and 1,300ft ascent per hour. These are fairly generous, and should allow you the occasional stop to admire the view, look at the map, take photographs, or recover your breath. They do not allow for protracted lunch stops! Extra time has been allowed if the going is difficult, and vice versa.

CLIMATE AND WEATHER

The climate of the east and southeast of Ireland, like that of the whole island, is shaped by two factors, the westerly atmospheric circulation, and the proximity of the Atlantic Ocean. These factors interact to give us westerly winds, mild damp weather and a small temperature range throughout the year.

Although the weather is very variable, certain climatic features seem to occur with some regularity. During December and January, there is a well-established low pressure system over the Atlantic, producing depressions which move rapidly eastwards bringing strong winds and abundant frontal rain. By late January the cold anti-cyclonic weather centred over Europe may be extending westwards into Ireland giving dry, cold spells, eminently suitable for hill walking. From February to June the cold European anti-cyclones tend to produce the driest period of the year. Towards late June or early July the pressure rises over the ocean and falls over the continent, initiating a westerly, damp airflow over Ireland. Cloud cover, humidity and rainfall increase and thunder becomes more prevalent, especially during the warmer periods of August. Cold northerly air may bring active depressions in late August and September, but these can be interrupted by spells of anti-cyclonic weather. In October and November rain-bearing westerlies predominate, though an incursion of anti-cyclonic conditions can bring blue skies and pleasant walking conditions. The prevailing winds are south-westerly and westerly, but winds from the north and east may occur with anti-cyclonic conditions. The winds are lightest from June to September, and strongest from November to March.

May tends to be the sunniest month with around six hours per day, falling away through June to four and a half hours per day in July.

As noted above, the spring is the driest part of the year, and though the ground underfoot is still very wet from the autumn and winter rains, March, April and May are perhaps the best months for walking.

In general rainfall decreases as one moves east, though this tendency is hardly noticeable in the mountain areas. Snow is uncommon in our maritime climate, rarely persisting for long, even at high level, though in some winters it may lie for several weeks in high north-facing coombes and gullies.

Looking more closely at the east, we find the highest average annual rainfall near the highest peaks and along the ridges connecting them. Near Lugnaquilla the average rainfall is about 2,400mm and near Kippure it is about 2,000mm. This compares with 700mm in Dublin City, about 800mm on the plains of Kildare and about 900mm along the Wicklow coast. There is no significant tendency for the western slopes to be wetter than the eastern slopes. In general, rainfall increases with elevation above sea level. However, deep narrow valleys in the mountains (e.g. Glenmalure) experience nearly as much rain as the mountains surrounding them. Average rainfall varies from month to month. In the Wicklow Mountains, December and January are the wettest months and April and June the driest. An idea of this annual variation is given by the monthly averages (in mm) for the Wicklow Gap over the period 1941–70.

Jan.	Feb.	Mar.	Apr.	May.	June.	July.	Aug.	Sept.	Oct.	Nov.	Dec.
219	150	117	134	108	108	120	151	176	181	195	243

However, don't let this put you off; armed with waterproof clothing even a showery day can be very pleasant between downpours. Remember the saying — 'rain before seven, sun before eleven,' which is very true of the mountains in this area.

Looking specifically at the southeastern counties, we find that the mountains receive an average 1,800 to 2,500mm (72 to 100 inches) of rain per annum, mainly from September through to January. The lower hills, particularly those of north Tipperary and Laois/Offaly receive from 1,200 to 2,000mm (48 to 80 inches) annually, whilst the lowland area tends to attract half that recorded in the mountains.

To fully appreciate the way that the high ground attracts the rain one has only to stand in bright sunshine on the plains of the area and see how often the mountains are wreathed in clouds. To further stress the necessity for guarding against the weather in these hills, it should be noted that there are on average 175 to 200 'wet' days annually, these being days on which at least 1mm of rain falls. Some consolation may be gained, however, from the fact that there are less than 90 days per annum without sunshine which suggests that many of the wet days also have their brighter periods.

EAST
David Herman

INTRODUCTION

My first memories of the Wicklow Mountains date from when I was about six. At that impressionable age I remember striding proudly and confidently down to Lough Dan — and being dragged tired and cranky all the way back. Nevertheless, in spite of (because of?) such early impressions it is 'only' in the last 25 years — thus leaving a yawning gap of 20 — that I have really got to know the Wicklow Mountains and it is as recently as the last ten that I have set foot in the Blackstairs.

In that quarter century the popularity of hill walking has increased in quantum leaps. Where once one could wander without meeting a soul, now, even on weekdays, it is unusual not to meet someone. As for Sundays . . . well, up to 50 or even 60 people might be out in one group and several large groups might be encountered in the course of a day's walking. Shades of Dublin's O'Connell Street! It would be mean-minded not to welcome this great increase in numbers even if it leads to paths being eroded and the remoteness of the hills being lost. After all, apart from the obvious fact that hillwalking is a healthy and participative (and mercifully, non-sponsored) recreation, the people who walk the mountains are the people who enjoy and appreciate them. They are the people who will protect the mountains and our environment generally and who will ultimately make it clear to our political masters that, yes, we do care or put more crudely, that there are votes 'in them thar hills'.

Never was this message of conservation in greater need of being proclaimed from the hill-tops. Not to put a tooth in it: *in general* we as a nation do not care much about our environment. As the inimitable travel writer, Dervla Murphy, once wrote (I paraphrase, I hope not too exaggeratedly): how can people who are surrounded by such natural beauty as we are be content to live in the midst of squalor? The litter on our streets, the sore thumbs of 'haciendas' rawly and incongruously perched on our hill-tops, and the rubbish dumped on our country roads are all manifestations of the same malaise. Too many of us do not care.

Yet all is not gloom. A most hopeful sign is the recent establishment of a National Park in the Wicklow Mountains — above all areas in the Republic, the most threatened by 'development' and deterioration. This is a real indication that we are prepared to protect a fragile and precious heritage. As someone who has pleaded for this for some years I welcome it most warmly. If this area is given the same high degree of protection as the other National Parks in Ireland — and I am sure it will be — we can look forward to the conservation, indeed the enhancement, of the area's beauty and of its amenity and scientific value.

There is one other consequence of the increased numbers walking the hills that I must regretfully mention. That is the pressure that great numbers of hill walkers put on farmers. We must not be surprised if farmers, especially those close to Dublin, consider themselves under siege. Litter is left strewn around for livestock to eat, fence wire is stood upon, stone walls knocked down, sheep harassed and killed by stray dogs. Of course the average hill walker though not entirely blameless is not responsible for all this, but someone is, and it is asking a lot of farmers to differentiate between responsible hill walkers and uncouth yobbos. We are all likely to be tarred with the one brush: trespassers and destructive trespassers at that.

It would help greatly to defuse tension if statutory rights of way were to be established from motorable roads through farmland to open country above but given the slow pace of legislative change here and the probable opposition — shortsighted opposition I would suggest — of land-owners, I cannot see this development occurring in the near future. In the meantime please take great care in or near enclosed fields. Study the Country Code given earlier. And if you are informed that you are trespassing go politely and without further ceremony.

Having said all this it is necessary to add an important and I hope reassuring rider. Though difficulties are understandably worst near Dublin, away from the city relations between farmers and hill walkers are much more amicable. Country people are almost invariably friendly and would appreciate a greeting and a few words of chat. Don't pass by in surly silence.

It is usual in the introduction to guide books to suggest modestly that the routes given are only a selection and that the user of the guide should use the book as a base for further exploration. And it's true of this guide. One of the great attractions of Irish mountains — and I say this in particular to overseas visitors — is that the terrain generally encourages a wide wandering. Once you reach the uplands you can wander more or less where you will. It's all waiting for *you* to explore!

Lastly I would like to thank my wife Mairin Geraty for walking many of the routes with me over the years and for her forthright comments on sloppiness in my prose (remaining sloppiness is of course my responsibility). I would also like to thank Joss Lynam, who asked me to co-author this book and who as ever gave, with his usual good humour, his time unstintingly and his expert advice ungrudgingly.

Access and Accommodation
Access by Car   We will, we hope, be excused if we describe access to the Wicklow Mountains, the area which is likely to be most difficult to access, almost entirely from the viewpoint of the Dublin-based walker. If you don't start from the capital there are few problems of access that the appropriate maps won't solve.

For the eastern side take the N11 to Kilmacanoge, turning right here onto the R755 for the Lough Tay/Lough Dan area, Glendalough and Glenmalure. The alternative route along the eastern flank is to take the R117 to Enniskerry, a scenic but narrow road which takes you through the spectacular defile of the Scalp.

The Military Road (designated R715 north of Sally Gap) is a high-level scenic route which runs the entire length of the Wicklow Mountains. For a quick exercise-free introduction to these mountains the Military Road to Glenmalure is unbeatable. Incidentally, it has the highest point of tarmac in Ireland (excluding cul-de-sacs) at 525m/1,724ft just north of Sally Gap.

For the western side take the N81 to or through Blessington. This road has good views of Pollaphuca Reservoir and the hills on the west of the Wicklow Mountains.

There are two *high-level east-west roads*. The more northerly is the Sally Gap road (R759) which runs from the R755 in the east past the dramatically beautiful Lough Tay area and crosses the Military Road at Sally Gap. From here it descends gradually to the N81 near Kilbride. The more southerly is the Wicklow Gap Road (R756) which runs from Glendalough, reaches its highest point (478m/1,567ft) close to Tonelagee and then descends parallel to the King's River by-passing Hollywood to reach the N81.

A general point. It is regrettable to have to say that you should leave no valuables visible, better you should leave no valuables at all, in cars parked anywhere in the Wicklow Mountains. In recent years there have been numerous break-ins to cars even in remote carparks.

Train and Bus Services   DART services to Bray are frequent and inexpensive but the only other possibly useful train service is that to Rathdrum. Dublin Bus provide a good service to many places in or near the Wicklow (and Dublin) Mountains. Those to Ballyknockan (65 bus route), Barnacullia (44B), Blessington (65), Bohernabreena (49A), Donard (65), Enniskerry (44), Glencullen (44B), Rockbrook (47A), and Shop River west of Enniskerry (85) are particularly useful but check times as some services are very infrequent.

There is also a privately operated bus service run by the St Kevin's Bus Company. The route is from St Stephen's Green West, Dublin to Glendalough taking in Kilmacanoge, Roundwood and Laragh. Details from the company at Roundwood, Co. Wicklow (phone 01-818119).

One last point for those using public transport. In general, if you are based in Dublin, it will be better for your peace of mind to walk northwards rather than south. This is because the bus service is more frequent nearer the city, that is, at the north of the range. It is easy enough to catch that solitary long-distance bus in the morning when you can judge your time accurately; then you can avail of the frequent local bus service in the evening when you can't.

Irish Bus (Bus Eireann) provincial bus services go to Blessington, Annalecky Cross (for Donard) and Baltinglass on the west of the Wicklow Mountains, Kilmacanoge and Rathdrum on the east; and Bagenalstown (Muine Bheag), Bunclody, Kiltealy and Graiguenamanagh for the Blackstairs. Check times carefully beforehand as none of these services is frequent.

Accommodation   If you prefer somewhere a little more peaceful than Dublin, there is plenty of accommodation in Blessington in the west, and more limited accommodation in many towns and villages in other mountain areas in Wicklow. Enniscorthy, Borris, Bunclody, Bagenalstown (Muine Bheag) and Graiguenamanagh are good bases from which to explore the Blackstairs. There are, of course, isolated houses in the countryside offering accommodation. Details of most hotel, guesthouse and farmhouse accommodation are given in brochures issued by Bord Failte Eireann (Irish Tourist Board).

So to the more modest. There are seven youth hostels in or near the mountains. Serving the northwest is Baltyboys (986 110), delightfully located on a peninsula on Pollaphuca reservoir but a little far from the hills. Further east are Knockree (192 150) and Glencree (140 179), both in Glencree. Glendalough is suitable for exploring the central area of Wicklow. Further south are Ballinclea (961 952) in the Glen of Imaal and Glenmalure (057 947), which is a small remote hostel and not always open. Lastly Aghavannagh (060 874) is at the southern end of the Military Road. To avail of hostel accommodation you have to be a member of a national youth hostel organisation. It is also advisable to book in advance. Further details available from An Oige, 39 Mountjoy Square, Dublin 1 (phone 01-363111).

Lastly, spartan types might consider camping. The only camping site near the mountains is at Roundwood. Nevertheless it is possible to camp almost anywhere but please ask the landowner's permission first. This injunction does not apply if you intend camping on bleak mountain tops!

Geology

The structure of the mountains should not be dismissed as being of merely academic interest to the walker. The type of rock in a region largely determines the terrain, is the basic material for the soil which develops above it, and so influences the vegetation and ultimately the animal life. Of course, vegetation and animal life are influenced by geology to only a limited degree, climate being the major factor. A knowledge of the geology of an area, however, provides a good indication of its other fundamental characteristics.

Standing on Bray Head, or Howth Head further north, the observer will be struck by the contrast between the hills along the eastern seaboard and those further west forming the crest of the range. The hills on the east are small but craggy and precipitous knobs and those to the west higher, but with gentle softly-rounded domes.

The explanation for this and similar contrasts lies in the nature and history of the rock types present in the mountain area. The most ancient rocks of the range belong to the Cambrian period (360 million years ago) and are exposed in an irregular, roughly triangular, area of northeast Co. Wicklow and southeast Co. Dublin. The peaks in this area are formed of highly resistant green and purple quartzites and have a characteristic bumpiness. In the lower lands lie beds of slate, quartz and sandstone. All these ancient rocks have been so twisted and contorted, broken and eroded through a period long even in geological terms that their complete history has never been deciphered and undoubtedly never will be. In spite of the local assumption which attributes these rocks to volcanic action — and looking at the sharp cone of Great Sugar Loaf this does not seem unreasonable — all these rocks were laid in fact at the bottom of a shallow sea.

In later times, during the Ordovician period, another deeper sea stretched across what is now Ireland, depositing beds of sedimentary rocks — shales, slates and sandstones — on its floor. When these rocks were eventually exposed to the air — due to the lifting of the ocean floor or the sinking of the sea — a subdued plain lay where the mountains of the east of Ireland now rise.

This terrain, with the central mountain core as yet unborn, existed for about 200 million years. Then molten lava, responding to some immense subterranean disturbance, welled up in a great northeast to southwest belt from below the older Ordovician rocks, forcing them into an enormous arch above it and completely altering the zone of Ordovician rock with which it came into contact. Eventually the lava cooled and solidified into the familiar granite of today — by far the largest granite area in this island. The Ordovician arch has almost completely weathered away, exposing the granite underneath in turn to the relentless assault of the elements.

Granite, in spite of its proverbial hardness, is particularly susceptible to chemical weathering: hence the rounded domes of the central granite massif. The zone of former Ordovician rock which came into contact with the molten lava was metamorphised into a flinty, flaky rock called mica-schist. The rock gives rise to a line of sharp hills and ridges along the granite border. These are more prominent in the east than the west, where the granite plunges more steeply below the Ordovician strata.

The mica-schist contact zone contains ores of lead, copper and iron, which were mined in the eighteenth and nineteenth centuries. The evidence of these workings — slag heaps, smelting houses, workers' dwellings, even rusting antiquated machinery — litters parts of the valleys of Glenmalure, Glendalough and Glendasan in an unlovely tangle. Fortunately for us, the workings were never on a very large scale and the scars are not very extensive.

The events so far described occurred hundreds of millions of years ago but the first Ice Age (there were at least two in Ireland) began only a million years ago and the last retreated north a mere 10,000 years ago. Since the latter was predominant in determining the present appearance of the mountains of the east, let us look at it now.

At its greatest extent a vast ice-sheet, similar to the polar ice-caps of today, covered most of the Irish lowlands. Above it the bulk of the mountains protruded like icebergs above a polar sea, but they did not escape the intense cold. At the onset of this Ice Age snow accumulated year after year, firstly in the higher, more sheltered eastern slopes of the hills and secondly, in similarly sheltered nooks and crannies everywhere in the mountains. After many years two great ice-fields formed — one from Glenmacnass to the wild country northeast of Sally Gap, the other from Lugnaquilla to the Wicklow Gap. At the same time the ice and snow in the sheltered nooks were carving out the corries of today. These are huge natural amphitheatres, great 'armchairs' complete with 'back,' 'arm-rests,' and 'seat' — the seat usually occupied by a lake. They are best displayed at both Lough Brays, Powerscourt Deerpark, and the two Prisons of Lugnaquilla. Eventually, from ice-field and corrie, the great mass of ice began to move off downhill as mountain glaciers, rivers of ice and snow carrying rocks, boulders and other debris.

It is necessary at this point to compare an unglaciated river valley with a glaciated one. A stream in its upper reaches wends its way between mountain spurs, carving out a channel shaped in cross-section like a shallow V. Now suppose a glacier invades such a valley. Because the glacier is so rigid and inflexible it gouges out a path straight down the valley, deepening it from a V into a U and shearing off the mountain spurs. When the glacier finally disappears a straight flat-bottomed valley with precipitous sides has been carved out.

Glenmalure illustrates some typical features of a glacial valley. Here the top of the U-valley is at about 1,100ft, indicated by a sudden change of slope and an irregular line of assorted boulders ('erratics') deposited from the top of the glacier. Above 1,100ft is the remnant of the V-valley; below, cliffs or very steep ground slope down to the flat valley floor of the Avonbeg River. Because the glacier has lowered this valley floor, the valleys of streams tributary to the Avonbeg, which have not been glaciated, are now high above it. These tributary valleys are called 'hanging valleys' and their streams plunge into Glenmalure as waterfalls. The valley of the Carrawaystick Brook is a typical hanging valley.

The moraine is another common glacial phenomenon occurring in Glenmalure. As already mentioned, a glacier transports all sorts of rubble as it grinds forward — boulders, rocks, sand and gravel. But whenever it halts all the rubble is carried forward to the tongue and dumped there in a long irregular line spanning the valley. The barracks at Drumgoff (Glenmalure) stand on a moraine, as does the Round Tower at Glendalough. The sandpits around Blessington and the hummocky country near Annamoe are also moraines, but were deposited under somewhat different conditions to those described.

As the climate ameliorated towards the end of the last Ice Age a dramatic physical feature was added to the landscape. This is the glacial spillway, best seen at the Scalp, the Glen of the Downs and the Hollywood Glen, but also elsewhere along the eastern and western flanks of the hills. It originated when, with the improving climate, vast quantities of snow and ice melted and huge lakes formed which were hemmed in between the ice-sheets on the plains and the mountain ridges of the hills. Eventually, the rising waters spilled over at the lowest point in the surrounding hills, cutting enormous gashes through them. Their characteristic shape means that they can be easily identified from the contour lines on the map.

Although all areas of the east, as indeed nearly all areas of Ireland, show the effects of glaciation, these effects are more prominent on the east of the range. For example, one of the most pleasant features of the mountain area is the contrast between the deep, narrow, straight glens of the east, which are highly glaciated, and the lightly glaciated, shallow open basins of the west which carry the upper reaches of the Slaney, the Liffey and their tributaries. It is to the Ice Age that we owe these and other contrasts, which have added so much the beauty of the hills.

Flora and Fauna

I now move on to the plant, bird and animal life of the mountains. I have tried to keep the summary brief but at the same time to give the casual reader an idea of what constitutes the flora and fauna of the area. I have also tried to mention items which he or she may come across while walking in these mountains.

Flora   The dominant character of the mountains of the east is formed by the forest plantations. Great zones of colour sweep the hillside contours giving suitable contrast to otherwise bleak mountain scenery. The main coniferous components of the area are the larch, which is soft green in spring and summer but pale and yellow in autumn, mingled with the dark greens of Sitka spruce and Corsican pine, and with belts of blue-green Scots pine, which has a reddish, gaunt and flattopped appearance in maturity. Occasional patches of silver fir, boasting large resin-coated cones, are a feature of Djouce Woods.

The native trees of Ireland are few in number and are well described in Beth-Luis-Nion's tree alphabet. Birch, rowan, ash, alder, hawthorn and holly are fairly common on the mountainside. They are of great importance as sources of food and shelter both for bird and insect life. Occasionally stands of aspen are encountered, in places such as the approach to Lugnaquilla above the Fraughan Rock Glen in Glenmalure. But the tree of prime importance in Wicklow is the oak (*Quercus robur*). It is limited to areas such as the Glen of the Downs and a few specimens are found in the Devil's Glen, Glencree and on the approaches to Lough Dan and Lough Tay. It is within an oak forest that one quickly learns to appreciate the forest environment. Oak galls with their larva inside, moss and lichen growth on stems (indicators of low air pollution), leaf galls and consequently heavy leaf litter which makes underfoot conditions pleasant, all add together to make a walk in this type of environment a most memorable experience. Plants within the oak domain vary from climbers, such as honeysuckle, to bulbs, such as the bluebell. On the fringe, primroses sometimes occur with a sprinkling of the invading rhododendron. In a native environment the introduction of aliens such as the rhododendron can lead to complete imbalance with natural regenerating tree and shrub species being suppressed.

The mountain terrain is a very bleak and difficult site for the development of a plant community. Constant wind, heavy rainfall, poor soil and an ever-increasing sheep population all limit plant life. Many areas of the mountains are covered by ling (*calluna*) heather (*Erica*), giving a characteristic purple tinge to the hills during August and September. As this plant gets older, vast frameworks of woody stems are produced. Ultimately controlled burning is carried out, which leads to fresh regrowth the following spring, and provides a welcome bite for the sheep. However, overzealous grazing or burning can lead to invasion by bracken. With its brittle stem and vast hoards of midges and flies most walkers are only too familiar with this plant. An annual, it dies back each winter, often making winter walking a more pleasant pastime.

The poor peatland soils on top of gentle bedrock are lacking in nitrogen, an essential element in plant development. Plants adapt in different ways to cope with this problem. Some have the ability to fix atmospheric nitrogen, such as alder, broom and gorse. Others have become more ingenious, namely the sundew. Its tiny leaves are modified to form a trap for unsuspecting insects and are as deadly as a spider's web. A sticky exudation covers each life. Insects that are attracted alight on the leaves, which move inwards to envelop the prey and digest the body fluids by enzymes. Protein is broken down into amino acid and nitrogen. The valley area surrounding the Raven's Glen is a very good one in which to find examples, but you need to be observant. The best time is about mid-July.

While the mountain flora is distinctly poor, due to height and exposure, certain unusual plants are to be found on Lugnaquilla, including clubmoss. Its scaly green silky stems are a sure indicator that you are high up on the mountain. London Pride (*Saxifraga umbrosa*), a rare Pyrenean plant, has also been found in this location. At lower altitudes, especially in the Sally Gap and on the approach to Kippure, purple loosestrife, with its bright purple plumes, can be seen in combination with bog cotton. The Upper Lake at Glendalough is also an area of botanical interest: white waterlilies grow in the calm water near the shoreline and a belt of Scots pines flanks the shore. Here witches brooms occur. These are caused by an insect feeding on the growing shoots of pine trees. The cells react by forming a tumour-like growth, which has a twisted, contorted habit and grows very slowly.

Fauna   The fauna of the mountains of the east is quite varied despite the increasing disturbance caused by the motorised public, who seem to

drive their vehicles further from the county roads each year. This move-
ment of people and their associated picnic waste has resulted in an
increase in the populations of the raven (*Corvus corax*) and the hooded
crow (*Corvus corone cornix*) due to the increased food supply. But the
advantages of human disturbance are outweighed by the disadvantages.
Each year more habitat is being destroyed and so we are losing different
species from particular areas year by year.

In the lower areas and in the vicinity of agricultural land one may find
the fieldfare (*Turdus pilaris*) and mistle thrush (*Turdus viscivorus*) among
the birds normally associated with suburban gardens. In addition, a common sight is that of a kestrel (*Falco tinnunculus*) hovering for long periods
before suddenly swooping on some prey such as a fieldmouse (*Sylvaemus
sylvaticus*). The starling (*Sturnus vulgaris*), while in small groups during
the summer months, can, with the advent of winter and swelled in numbers by immigrants, be seen in huge flocks numbering several thousand
moving en masse from field to field. The jackdaw (*Corvus monedula*) and
rook (*Corvus frugilegus*) behave in a similar manner. Starling roosts are
found in some coniferous forests, where the stench of droppings can be
sufficient to nauseate even the hardiest of walkers. The robin (*Erithacus
rubecula*) although normally associated with suburban back gardens, is a
common sight in the diverse habitat of our woodlands. In common with
the robin, the great tit (*Parus major*), coal tit (*Parus ater*), blue tit (*Parus
caeruleus*) and the long tailed tit (*Aegithalso candatus*) share the habitat,
generally moving about in small groups and drawing attention to themselves by constant twittering. The pheasant (*Phasianus colchicus*) will most
likely betray its presence by a sudden vertical take-off accompanied by
loud whirring wind noises. Another bird of the woodlands, with interesting
feeding habits, is the tree creeper (*Certhia familiaris*), which climbs up trees
spirally in short bursts with its stiff tail pressed against the bark, while
using its thin curved bill to search for insects in bark crevices.

Among gorse and heather one may find the linnet (*Acanthis cannabina*),
redpoll (*Acanthis flammea*) and whinchat (*Saxicola rubetra*). In summer the
meadow pipit (*Anthus pratensis*) and the skylark (*Alanda arvensis*), with its
musical outpourings at great height, move to the hills from lower ground.
The twite (*Acanthis flavirostris*) is found in this region also, but can be
confused with the linnet.

Associated with streams and ponds are the grey wagtail (*Motacilla
cinerea*), dipper (*Cinclus cinclus*) and perhaps, in quieter waters, the king-
fisher (*Alcedo atthis*) and grey heron (*Ardea cinerea*), the latter standing stock
still while preying upon frogs and smaller varieties of fish.

Higher up on the heather moors the most common bird in former
times was the red grouse (*Lagopus lagopus scoticus*) but, with the decline in
proper grouse moor management, numbers have dropped to seriously
low levels. Also in this habitat one can expect to observe the hen harrier
(*Circus cyaneus*), one-time predator of the red grouse, hooded crow and

raven. The rarest bird of prey in the region is the peregrine falcon (*Falco peregrinus*), which is making a slow comeback to the wilder areas, but at the moment its haunts are closely-guarded secrets.

It is probable that the red fox (*Vulpes vulpes*) is the most talked about animal in rural areas. It has been the scourge of both sheep farmers and gamekeepers alike. However the mink (*Mustela vison*) has now achieved some notoriety in this field and has the reputation of a fierce and wanton killer. It fits into an ecological niche between that of the otter (*Lutra lutra*) and the stoat (*Mustela erminea*). The mink has been largely responsible for the decimation of both the coot (*Fulica atra*) and moorhen (*Gallinula chloropus*) populations of streams and ponds in the eastern half of the country. All the same, it does useful work in keeping the rat (*Rattus norvegicus*) population down to a manageable level. The rabbit (*Oryctolagus cuniculus*) has long been a menace to tillage farmers because of its voracious appetite and reproductive capacity. Nowadays its numbers are much reduced owing to the inroads of myxomatosis.

The state forests, boring as they may look from the outside, and from the inside to some eyes as well, do provide a very diverse habitat for many animals and birds. In the forests where Scots pine and larch are found in sizeable quantity one is sure to observe the red squirrel (*Scuirus vulgaris*) on the ground or streaking up the trunk of a tree. The grey squirrel (*Neoscuirus carolinensis*) is also found, but at present is confined to the northern part of the region.

It is possible to observe the woodmouse (*Sylvaemus sylvaticus*) in most types of woodland. Despite being associated with back gardens, the hedgehog (*Erinaceous europaeus*) is also present and can be seen, mainly at dusk, searching for food in the form of earthworms (*Lumbricus spp*) and the young of the woodmouse and other small rodents. The badger (*Meles meles*) is a common resident of both coniferous and deciduous woodland, making elaborate setts wherever the soil is dry and least compacted.

On open moorland one is likely to find the blue hare (*Lepus timidus*) and on, or adjacent to, grassland the larger brown hare (*Lepus capensis*). It is in this particular vegetation zone that the largest of our wild mammals, the deer (*Cervus spp*), is located. In order to eliminate confusion as regards the deer in Co. Wicklow it should be noted that all the deer in upland zone are hybrids of the red deer (*Cervus elaphus*) and the Japanese sika deer (*Cervus nippon*). Some, especially those in the Turlough Hill area, show characteristics of the Japanese sika deer and are termed 'sika-like'. A small number of fallow deer (*Dama dama*) can be found in the Ashford-Rathdrum area. The only other animal population of note found wild in this region is the feral goat (*Capra spp*) which arose from the domestic goat either by escaping or by deliberate releasing of unwanted animals. There are several herds, the one at Glendalough being the best known.

Key Map

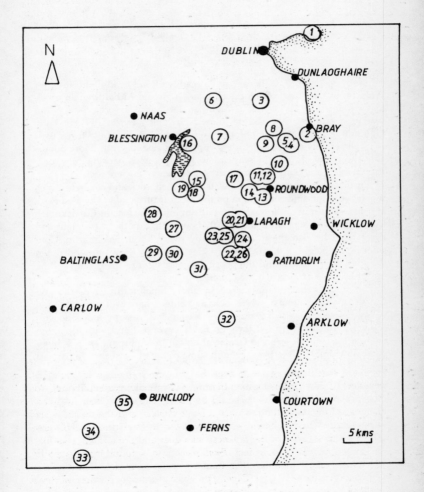

N

DUBLIN

DUNLAOGHAIRE

①

⑥   ③

● NAAS

BLESSINGTON   ⑯   ⑦   ⑧   ② BRAY
⑨   ⑤,④

⑩

⑰   ⑪,⑫

⑮   ⑭   ⑬ ● ROUNDWOOD
⑲ ⑱

⑳,㉑ LARAGH   ● WICKLOW
㉘
㉗   ㉓,㉕   ㉔
㉒,㉖   ● RATHDRUM
㉙ ㉚
BALTINGLASS ●   ㉛

● CARLOW

㉜   ● ARKLOW

㉟ ● BUNCLODY   ● COURTOWN

㉞   ● FERNS   5 kms

㉝

19

1. HOWTH HEAD

The tiny rocky hills of Howth Head and its nearby seacliffs and secluded coves are a favourite area for Dubliners, and no wonder. Here, within a few miles of the city centre is an area, almost an island, with an atmosphere and terrain quite different to the city's bustling streetscapes. Nevertheless it is partly a built-up area and this precludes any sense of wild remoteness. Better accept it for what it is, a type of suburban wilderness.

Howth is well served by DART and the 31 bus route. If travelling by car, park near the DART station.

From the harbour, walk east up Balscadden Road heading for the Cliff Walk. Along the first stretch the cliffs are high and forbidding: an excellent area for seabirds nesting in 'high-rise flats', with the occasional patrol sweeping out over the sea or towards Ireland's Eye. After the Baily Lighthouse on a tiny promontory down on the left, the route turns west as imperceptibly as it has already swung from east to south. More noticeably the rocky cliffs yield seaward to grassy slopes backing tiny rock-strewn inlets and bony upward-reaching fingers of ancient rock.

Further along watch out for a wall of seashell, rock and concrete which will be your guiding companion on the right. It turns inland at Red Rock and here you must follow a steep path uphill to tarmac at Carrickbrack Road. Turn left here, walk 250m/270yds or so to a path on the right and climb from here to the top of a nearby rocky knoll, Shielmartin. Considering its height, not much over 150m/500ft, the views up and down the coast are excellent and the possibility of a sight of the distant rolling Mournes lends a touch of added interest.

Descend to the cottage tucked in under Shielmartin, cross the golf course following a line of white rocks and enter a narrow heavily wooded valley between two rocky ridges. At its far end pass by a second golf course on the left, turn left through fields beyond it and with a playing field on the right descend to tarmac at Balkill Road. From here it is but a short downhill stroll to base through some of the more attractive parts of Howth.

Distance: 10.5km/6.5miles. Ascent:150m/500 ft. Walking time: 3 hours.

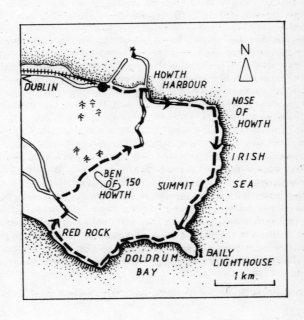

N

DUBLIN

HOWTH
HARBOUR

NOSE
OF
HOWTH

IRISH

BEN
OF 150
HOWTH

SUMMIT

SEA

RED ROCK

DOLDRUM
BAY

BAILY
LIGHTHOUSE

1 km.

Reference OS Maps: Dublin street plan (1:20,000) or Dublin District
(1:63,360).

2. BRAY HEAD

It is probably not fully appreciated that height is not a prerequisite for an excellent mountain viewpoint. A low but well-placed vantage point can offer better views than a high summit hemmed in by dull shoulders. *Bray Head is an example: a varied and scenic panorama of indented coast, nearby shapely rocky hills and further away rolling domes of the whole northeast of the range, all from a mere 200m/650ft high. If you want to spend a half-day you could do a lot worse than sample the scenic and varied walking on lowly Bray Head.*

Bray is well served by DART and buses. Travellers by car can gain a little height by driving to the Strand Road and then following the inconspicuous signs for 'Scenic Car Park'.

From the start of the Cliff Walk climb by any convenient path to the Cross on the hummock which dominates the northern top. This is a rather unkempt and eroded stretch but do not be discouraged; better terrain awaits. At the Cross walk to a track running close to the next rocky hummock. And here I can reveal the great navigational simplicity of this walk: *all* turns from here on are left! So turn left onto the track and walk along a tiny plateau towards the South Top — an upland world of tiny rocky 'haystacks', rough gorse and bracken, the swelling ocean on one side, the small but impressive Sugar Loafs on the other. You might even be lucky enough to see the herd of feral goats whose stamping ground this is. All in all, quite a contrast to busy Bray so close at hand.

The South Top is out of bounds, so you must walk west down the track to a by-passed stretch of road, turn left here and turn left again onto the Bray-Greystones road. Fork left to keep on this road at the hamlet of Windgates, turn left towards the convalescent home, walk (quietly please!) through its carpark, take the path beyond and turn left onto the Cliff Walk.

The 2.5km/1.5miles back to Bray are dominated by the wrinkled waters of the ocean stretching away seemingly to infinity: its littoral of ancient rock; the myriads of kittiwakes, gulls, guillemots and shags which depend on it; its erosive power as evidenced by the abandoned railway tunnels. Man, perhaps mercifully, is not yet quite the measure of all things!

Distance: 8km/5miles. Ascent: 180m/600ft. Walking time: 2½ hours.

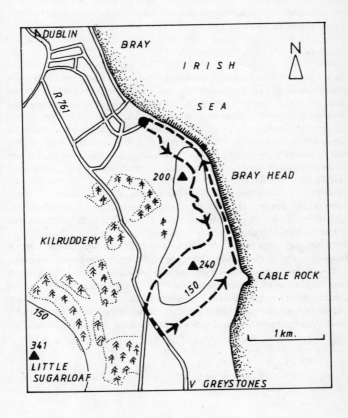

DUBLIN

BRAY

IRISH

SEA

R 761

N

BRAY HEAD

200

KILRUDDERY

240

CABLE ROCK

150

1 km.

150

341

LITTLE
SUGARLOAF

V GREYSTONES

Reference OS Maps: Dublin or Wicklow District (1:63,360) or Sheet 56
(1:50,000).

3. THREE ROCK AND FAIRY CASTLE

Over the southeast suburbs of Dublin a low plateau modestly rises. Its highest points are Fairy Castle and the granite tor-topped Three Rock and Two Rock. Given the close proximity of the entire plateau to the city the wonder is that anything worth walking remains. Yet there are some quite pleasant areas left, still preserving a sense of remoteness though so near the metropolis.

You can reach Barnacullia village (181 242) by car, about 1.5km/1mile south of Lamb Doyles pub on Woodside Road. The 44B bus serves Barnacullia but is infrequent. The more frequent 44 bus goes as far as Lamb Doyles. The 44B might be used in one direction though unlikely to be frequent enough to be used in both.

Walk back towards Dublin from the Blue Light pub, taking the first track on the left (west). At the first bend take a narrow path right off it and walk steadily uphill through a gorse and heather area which allows widening views over the city and towards the sea. Turn left at the first branch and follow this convoluted path to forest ahead. At the forest edge turn left and head towards Three Rock, a veritable pin-cushion of masts bristling just over the horizon. From Three Rock walk to Fairy Castle (538m/1,765ft), the highest point in the area. On this short stretch there is a plethora of paths and tracks to guide — or confuse — so a compass bearing may be prudent.

From Fairy Castle head for Two Rock, indicated by a heap of stones nearby on the horizon. This ragbag heap is emphatically *not* one of the Rocks of Two Rock; these noble granite tors lie disdainfully a little further on, across a forest fence.

We now enter the terrain of forest tracks and consequently of terribly tedious text. Here goes! Once across the fence, head downward east (not south) to a forest track, turn right (south) here and turn left at a forest corner beside the track to follow a clear wide firebreak downhill. Crossing a faint track, turn left again at a good forest track.

At the forest bar turn right, go right at the T below, pass a turning circle on the right (mentioned here only as a reassurance — don't head for it) and — here directions may be slightly relaxed — keep to the path and out of forest where there is a choice. At a well-surfaced gravelled track turn right (if you have any doubts about this, continue straight ahead and you will find the path you have been on quickly deteriorates). This track leads to tarmac, and a left turn and a walk of 1.5km/1mile will take you back to Barnacullia.

Distance: 6.5km/4miles. Ascent: 330m/1,100ft. Walking time: 2½ hours.

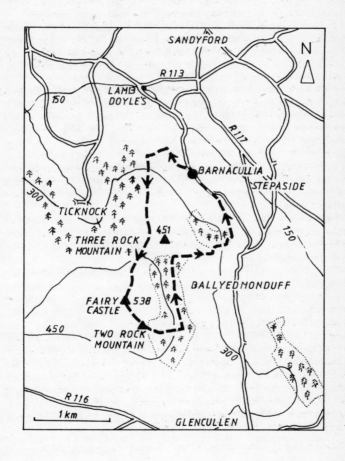

Reference OS Map: Dublin District (1:63,360).

4. LITTLE SUGAR LOAF

Little Sugar Loaf (341m/1,123ft), more an undulating ridge than a peak, runs north to south between Bray Head to the east and Great Sugar Loaf to the west, and gives fine views of both. Like them, it exhibits ancient jagged rock resulting in bold craggy outlines. All in all, it makes a delightful walk.

Go by car or bus to Kilmacanoge village on the N11. Travellers by bus will have to walk from here. Travellers by car (and those who had travelled by bus) should turn east in the village just south of R755 and proceed uphill for 1.3km/0.8miles to a patch of grass on the left (257 140).

Take the track (not the path to its left) from the parking place over a rough area of scattered trees to the south of the mountain. At one point the track degenerates to an unkempt path but persevere: as it dips under a power line it improves and joins a much more attractive track running south to north along the eastern side of the ridge. Turn left onto this track for a pleasant stroll, with a wooded area to your right and beyond it the bumpy 'haystacks' of Bray Head.

Where the track hairpins right and starts decisively downhill is the place to leave it. Cross the fence or wall on the left here, turn left and climb up the rocky shoulder towards the first of three tops. Anywhere along the high ground makes a good place for a rest. The views to both east and west — and they can be appreciated from the same spot — are excellent: Wicklow Head, Bray Head, Killiney and Howth thrusting towards the sea; Great Sugar Loaf rising magnificently to the west and overshadowing the rounded domes of the main range behind it. The return is south by a partly tumbled wall and a narrow fringe of trees. A few hundred yards along this wall turn right onto the original track of the day and return to the start.

Distance: 4km/2.5miles. Ascent: 180m/600ft. Walking time: 1½ hours.

5. GREAT SUGAR LOAF

Great (Big) Sugar Loaf exhibits an almost perfect cone from most directions; it has the classic 'mountain' profile as drawn by generations of artistically-inclined children. To avoid a relentless slog up its uniform and unsubtle slopes, this walk starts low in the village of Kilmacanoge thus concealing the full magnitude of the climb for as long as possible. However, if it's a wide view and not a walk that draws you, start from the carpark on Calary (235 119) and follow the multitudes!

Go by car or bus to Kilmacanoge 5km/3miles south of Bray on the N11. Start up the R755, taking a side road left opposite the church on the right. Keep straight on, following a minor road where this side road swings left and turn right at the house 'Redridge' on the left. Pass through the gate between two houses further up and continue upwards, Rocky Valley close below on the right. Ignoring the path running left at a lateral line of trees, carry on for a short distance until your track shows a disagreeable inclination to rise further. Turn sharply left here onto a path, and fork right further up, at which point the summit first appears, rearing impressively — and, hopefully, not too alarmingly — upwards.

Following what is once again a path, keep field boundaries on the right, and make a direct assault on the summit via wandering paths — or over heather when no other option seems likely to achieve this. It's a direct but sharp climb! Predictably the top of Great Sugar Loaf (501m/ 1,654ft) commands a wide array of mountains: Djouce close to the west with the massed hills of the northeast of the range to its left and right, Little Sugar Loaf and Bray Head with the sea behind to the east, and the long stretch of Calary Plateau to the south.

For the return you can make a direct approach towards Kilmacanoge over heaped rocks (watch your step at the start!) heading to the left of the obtrusive playing field as you descend. Beyond it you will hit tarmac and a left turn onto it will take you back to Kilmacanoge.

Distance: 6.5km/4miles. Ascent: 420m/1,400ft. Walking time: 2½ hours.

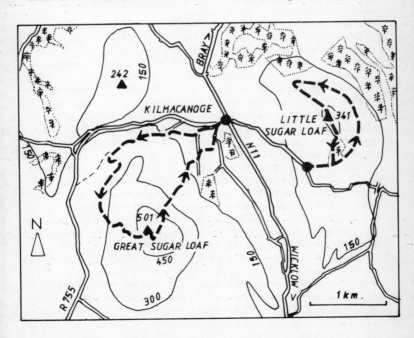

Reference OS Maps: Wicklow District (1:63,360) or Sheet 56 (1:50,000).

6. SEAHAN FROM STONE CROSS

A long spur of gently rolling but none the less scenic mountains runs from the border of Co. Wicklow northwest to the suburbs of Dublin, bounded on one side by lowlands and wooded hills and on the other by the glacial valley of Glenasmole. This walk encompasses the best of this area: climbing the spur from north to south and then descending by a track into Glenasmole.

One of a number of routes by car takes the N81 to Templeogue, then turns left over Templeogue Bridge and immediately right. Drive straight ahead for 8.4km/5.2miles, parking at Stone Cross (075 227), at a turn on the left near the top of a steep hill. This walk may also be organised using Dublin Bus route 49A (with alas a long road walk) or indeed by bicycle. From Stone Cross, take the side road south, passing through the gate on the left a few yards further on. Ascend the grassy hillside keeping somewhat to the right of the line which a direct assault on the slope would suggest. The reason for this is that you must find a narrow concealed path through the forest rising in massed and threatening ranks ahead. At the forest edge, and with the path now indubitably to the left, turn left and seek out the path at about 080 220.

Once you have found it, you can breathe easy because no more navigational problems arise until near the end. Walk up along the path — it's very muddy in places — to emerge on the northern slopes of Ballymorefinn Hill (515m/1,689ft) with a long stretch of uphill walking, forest on the right, upland pasture and the scenic Bohernabreena Reservoir on the left.

Seahan (648m/2,132ft) commands good views over the northwest of the range, the cairned Seefin to the south being particularly notable. A short descent and shorter ascent ends in the grassy mound of Corrig (618m/2,035ft), after which southward progress towards Seefingan is along a broad boggy ridge with the distinct cone of Great Sugar Loaf peeping unmistakably over the anonymous moorland closer at hand.

Seefingan (724m/2,364ft) is crowned by a huge tumulus and since there is a virtual plateau hereabouts, the tumulus in effect *constitutes* the summit. It is reached by climbing directly from the saddle point between Corrig and Seefingan and veering right at the crest of the hill on a path near the latter. The descent is along the Slade Brook reached by walking southeast a few hundred yards towards Kippure and then veering left downhill thus picking up the headwaters of the brook.

Keep to the left bank as you descend to reach a pleasant grassy track (along here note the stunted trees clinging precariously to the sheltered bank of the river — an interesting example of an ecological niche). Pass through a gate at the end of this track to reach the road. Turn left here and follow tarmac down to the main road running along the southwest side of the reservoir system. At the T-junction turn left again and walk steeply uphill to Stone Cross.

Distance: 16km/10miles. Ascent: 610m/2,000ft. Walking time: 5½ hours.

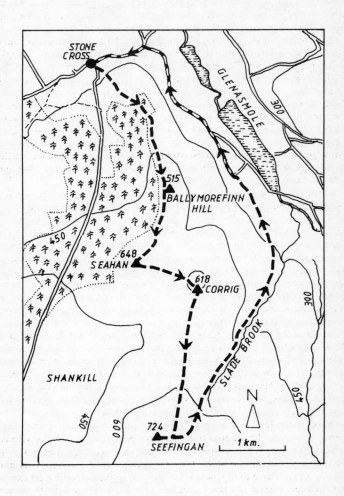

STONE CROSS

GLENASMOLE

300

515

BALLYMOREFINN HILL

450

648

SEAHAN

618

CORRIG

SLADE BROOK

300

SHANKILL

450

009

450

724

SEEFINGAN

N

1 km.

Reference OS Maps: Dublin District (1:63,360).

29

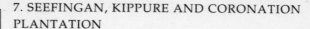

7. SEEFINGAN, KIPPURE AND CORONATION PLANTATION

This route combines some bleak and austere gently rolling mountain-side with the more intimate secluded river bank of the youthful River Liffey. The megalithic tombs on Seefin and Seefingan and the TV mast on Kippure exemplify ancient and modern worship customs, and on a severely practical note they are useful landmarks in a fairly blank terrain.

Take the N81 for 2.7km/1.7miles beyond Brittas, turning left here onto the R759. Drive onward on the R759 for 9km/5.5miles and park in Kippure Wood carpark on the left at 080 145. (Watch out for the inadequately sign-posted left turn followed shortly by a right 1.6km/1mile from the turn-off from the N81.) This route is also suitable for cyclists from Dublin.

From the carpark walk upstream without crossing the river, carrying on resolutely where the track succumbs. Crossing a fence (carefully) at the top of mature forest, continue upwards between the stream on the left and new forestry on the right. Once beyond the crossways fence at the upper end of the plantation, head directly half-left diagonally uphill to Seefin (*Sui Finn*, Seat of Finn: 621m/2,043ft).

Only at the enormous prehistoric burial chamber on the summit will you fully appreciate your position. Away across the plains of Kildare the cooling towers of Allenwood and even Portarlington may be visible while north and south the mountains of the northwest of the range peter out in the low hills on the Kildare border.

Seefingan (724m/2,364ft), a loftier version of Seefin and like it crowned by a prehistoric grave, is the next target. After it there is a long feature-less stretch terminating in Kippure, along the unfortunately unmarked county boundary. Along this stretch you have a choice of views towards Glenasmole to the north or over the Mullaghcleevaun range to the south, though neither direction is particularly exciting.

A soggy mound, unnamed on the maps, followed by a rise through black mud interspersed with startlingly green wedges leads to Kippure (? *Ciop mhor*, Great Place of Coarse Grass; 757m/2,475ft) the highest point in Co. Dublin. Its TV transmitter is evident, all too evident, for miles around so you will have no difficulty finding the peak though the surrounding terrain, an inverted pudding bowl, precludes good scenery except in the middle distance and beyond, and even here it is none too inspiring.

The next stage requires careful navigation. Take a bearing of about 220 degrees compass to reach a bridge on the R759 (as you descend aim for the scattered dark green trees at the eastern extremity of Coronation Plantation). Cross the road and walk down to the River Liffey, here a clear vibrant brook and a far cry from the sluggish mature river it becomes in the more familiar environment of Dublin.

The homeward stretch is a pleasant easy walk along the river. Keeping on the right bank, walk downstream, past (but do not cross) the bridge on the left across the Liffey, and ford the unbridged tributary beyond this bridge. Further down is an area of dense forest where you should keep close to the river. Just beyond this forest and with the walls of Kippure House ahead, turn right upwards through fields, pass through a gate onto the road and walk the 1km/0.5miles back to the start.

Distance: 14.5km/9miles. Ascent: 570m/1,900ft. Walking time: 5 hours.

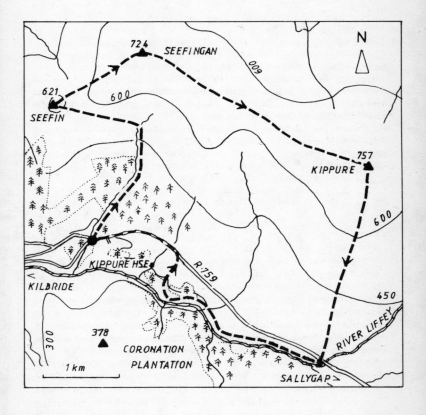

Reference OS Maps: Dublin or Wicklow District (1:63,360) or Sheet 56 (1:50,000).

8. GLENCULLEN

This walk is hard to title accurately in a word or two. It takes in a little of Glencree, and much of the northeast plateau near Dublin but the short valley of Glencullen is never far away — hence the title above. Too close to Dublin to escape its litter, unsuitable housing and other eyesores, Glencullen none the less retains a surprisingly rural atmosphere and the mountains to its north and south, though flat to the point of dullness, are sufficiently untamed to escape most of the problems evident lower down.

Take the Shop River variation of the 85 route from Enniskerry to its terminus west of Kilmalin (203 172). Decide the most suitable bus route for the Dublin end of the walk beforehand.

Walk west along the road from the terminus for about 1.5km/1mile to the Wicklow Way signpost at the entrance to Curtlestown Wood. Take the Way up through partly clear-felled forest to its top and, leaving the Way here, continue to Prince William's Seat (555m/1,825ft).

From here it is 'simply' a matter of following the ridge westward to Cruagh Mountain 6km/4miles away over terrain which slopes generally upward, along ditches and badly eroded paths — and the unobligingly invisible Wicklow-Dublin county boundary. The slightly ironic 'simply' mentioned above is because the ridge is so broad that it is easy to wander off it in bad weather; the only easily identifiable point is the tor close to the top of Knocknagun (163 186). All along here the views are quite good, the corries at Lough Bray being particularly noteworthy.

Glendoo, or rather the fence just beyond it, heralds the approach of Cruagh. Cruagh also has a fence immediately before its summit (such as it is), which is marked by a small cairn. From the summit, walk to the nearly 90 degree angle in the forest fence northeast of Cruagh, turn west and take the first wide path 250m/270yds from this angle directly into forest.

Turn right onto the forest track below and follow this track round a sharp vee. Finally take the first forest track off it — a sharp right — to reach tarmac almost opposite Tibradden carpark. (I apologise for this tedious recital of unfortunately necessary directions — alas, more follow. To divert all too briefly to the scenery: the forest terrain hereabouts is quite good of its type, scattered and felled trees giving pleasant glimpses of nearby mountainside.)

Cross the road to Tibradden carpark, where more forest tracks and inevitably further tedious directions re-commence. Walk to the end of the carpark and continue straight on. Turn right at the T and take the first forest *track* (not path) on the left. This will take you to a stake bearing a horse-shoe, a timely reassurance. Turn right uphill here and emerge from forest on the western shoulder of Tibradden. Fork right a little further on and walk along the top of the ridge, past a passage grave and granite tor, a route which gives good views south over Glencullen to the ridge traversed earlier in the day.

At the Wicklow Way signpost turn left along the Way, leaving it shortly to climb Fairy Castle, the highest point around (538m/1,765ft). In spite of this, the virtual plateau hereabouts means that the views are circumscribed. Continue downhill to Three Rock (451m/1,479ft) which has the dubious distinction of being one of the few unmistakable mountains on this walk — but only because of the numerous masts and blockhouses 'adorning' its summit plateau.

At Three Rock descend north, forest on the left, to a small stile about 822m/900yds down from the forest's upper edge. Take a secluded path left into forest here, and descend to Ticknock Road. From here walk to the bus; the choice being near bus routes that aren't frequent and frequent bus routes that aren't near.

Distance: 21km/13 miles. Ascent: 700m/2,300ft. Walking time: 7 hours.

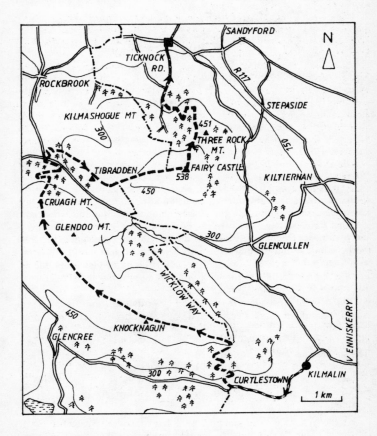

Reference OS Maps: Dublin District (1:63,360).

9. MAULIN AND THE TONDUFFS FROM CRONE

The south side of Glencree is dominated by Maulin. At 570m/1,871ft it is not the highest of the peaks around Glencree but it is certainly the most distinctive — the only one with pretensions to having a 'proper' conical peak. To the west, higher but more self-effacing, loom the Tonduffs, North and South, in effect one peak, or perhaps better described as a stretch of rolling moor-land which incidentally attains its highest point around here. Let's not forget the valleys, the shining glory of this whole area: the Deer Park into which plunges Powerscourt Waterfall, lonely Glensoulan above the Waterfall and the rocky slabs and tiny waterfalls of the stern Raven's Glen. All in all, a walk which although short still takes in quite a varied terrain.

Transport for this walk must be by car or bicycle. From Enniskerry take the road south past Powerscourt on the right, turning right at the T, 3.4km/2.1miles from Enniskerry. Park in Crone carpark (192 043) on the left, 3.8km/2.4miles from this T.

From the carpark take the main track, swing first left onto the Wicklow Way and follow it until further notice. An unlovely clear-felled area starts this stretch, then dense and all-encompassing forest follows until, when all seems lost, the forest relents and the close to despairing traveller emerges into the broad light of day, Deer Park at his or her feet. This first sight of the Deer Park is breathtaking: the deep bowl with its scattered trees, the mighty Powerscourt Waterfall ahead and behind it all the towering bulk of Djouce. No need to assimilate it all in one glance as this scene will be set before you, modifying only slowly, for the next 1.5km/1mile.

Eventually a band of forest obliterates the view; once through it the walker emerges back into open ground at a tumbled wall, Glensoulan and the upper Dargle on the left, the eastern shoulder of Maulin on the right. Leaving the Wicklow Way here the next task is to climb Maulin. This is easily done (or rather, easily navigated!) by following the wall to the crest of the shoulder and turning left (west) here onto a clear path to the summit. Maulin (*Malainn*, Hill Brow: 570m/1,871ft) is a fine viewpoint. Maybe among the rolling hills to the west you can discern the sharp distinctive rim of the corrie cut into Mullaghcleevaun?

The descent west again from Maulin towards the Tonduffs takes you down a couple of rocky steps, onto a boggy saddle, over an anonymous boggy shoulder labelled simply 1,944ft on the older maps, and then onto a steady boggy ascent to the Tonduffs, first the South and then the North. The separateness of the Tonduffs from each other, never great, has been lessened by the Ordnance Survey's 1:50,000 Sheet 56 which does not even accord each an individual contour line. However the south top has a large rock marking its summit and the north has a cairn, so some honour is retained.

From Tonduff North the walk continues into the impressive Raven's Glen. This involves a fairly steep descent to the east, avoiding rocky slabs and buttresses. Do not descend directly north to the forest edge as this is a nightmare terrain of greasy rocks, hidden crevices and slippery fallen branches.

Once more on level ground pick your way carefully between the stone wall on the left and a clear-felled area on the right as far as a forest track. Turn right here, take the left at the first fork and walk steadily downhill to Crone.

Distance: l0.5km/6.5miles. Ascent: 550m/1,800ft. Walking time: 4 hours.

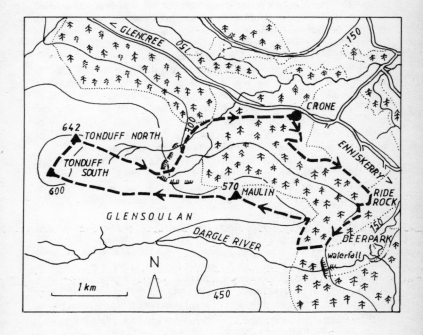

Reference OS Maps: Wicklow District (1:63,360) or Sheet 56 (1:50,000).

10. DJOUCE AND WAR HILL

Djouce is the mountain that dominates the west of the Calary Plateau: a high ridge reaching impressively south to north with a north-western spur culminating somewhat anti-climactically in War Hill. To the north of these hills Glensoulan carries the upper Dargle River which tumbles majestically into Powerscourt's Deer Park. This route takes in all this scenic and varied terrain in a short but demanding walk.

Drive to Enniskerry and take the road south, passing Powerscourt Gates on the right, towards Roundwood. About 6km/4miles from Enniskerry, park in the second carpark on the right (the first is set back from the road) at Djouce Woods (212 122).

Take the path from the carpark to the T, turn left and walk to the site of Paddock Pond, once a pleasant reservoir but, since its dam was washed away in 1986, an oozing foul-smelling swamp. Cross the near end, walk (hastily) along its west side and ascend into the trees beyond it, crossing a decrepit fence left where feasible.

With forest on the right, ascend to the crest where you will be greeted by a Wicklow Way signpost. Follow the Way uphill here towards Djouce, branch right (north) at the top of the ridge and walk to the summit of Djouce, easily recognisable because of its three rocky outcrops of mica-schist. Djouce (*Dubh ais*, Black Mountain: 725m/2,385ft) has a lofty and somewhat isolated position thus ensuring a wide and varied view of mountain, bogland, plain and even seascape, with nearby Maulin (except for the ubiquitous Sugar Loaf) the most easily recognisable peak.

From Djouce push west and then northwest, to the Coffin Stone, a curious name but a highly apt one when you observe the shape of the huge boulder crowning the assemblage. From here the remainder of the descent and a short ascent ends in War Hill (?*An bharr*, the Summit: 686m/2,250ft), a not very elegant mound.

North of War Hill lies the soggy headwaters of the Dargle, riven into the bogland sloping gently downward from the R115 (Military Road). To avoid the worst of this area head northeast from War Hill to the river and follow the right bank through a pleasant narrow valley downstream to the forest just above Powerscourt Waterfall. Continue downstream on a difficult path, over rocks, under branches and between muddy patches to open ground overlooking the Deer Park. From here follow a path, whose general trend is away from the waterfall, to the grassy basin below.

It really isn't far from here back to base — tortuous progress will, however, make it seem so. So let's go! Keeping to the right bank, walk downstream to the first tributary, then, keeping close to its bank — you will have to walk now on one side, now on the other — struggle upstream through a region of toppled trees to a low (2m/6ft high) but definite waterfall. Ascend the right (true) bank about here to a track and walk *downstream* to the first branch on the track. Turn right steeply uphill here, carry straight on at a cross tracks (it has a signpost) and turn right at the T higher up. First left off this, the initial path of the day, leads back to the car.

Distance: 13.5km/8.5miles. Ascent: 640m/2,100ft. Walking time: 5 hours.

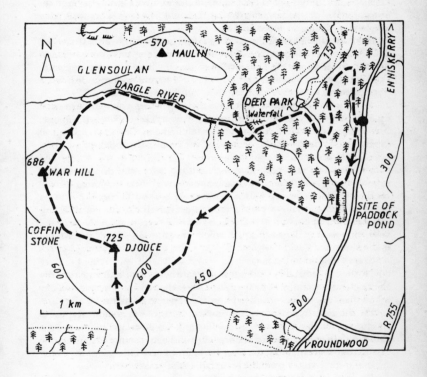

Reference OS Maps: Wicklow District (1:63,360) or Sheet 56 (1:50,000).

11. FANCY, COFFIN STONE AND DJOUCE

This walk might be fancifully described as a 'reverse' sandwich: the tasty meat on the outside with a slice of rather stodgy bread within. The scenic delights of the climb to Fancy yield to the boggy slog to the Coffin Stone. From Djouce on, however, the views are excellent and the underfoot conditions generally good.

Take the N11 to Kilmacanoge, 5km/3miles south of Bray. Turn right onto the R755 here and turn right again onto the R759 after a further 11km/7miles. Drive uphill for 3.2km/2miles and park near the large set of gate pillars on the left (at 172 064). This is Pier Gates. This walk may also be done using the St Kevin's bus.

From the pillars, walk the tarmacadam road down towards the valley floor along what must be one of the most spectacular motorable roads in the country: the great cliffs under Fancy directly ahead, bumpy Knockna-cloghoge to its left and a whole array of lovely mountains around with the purple heathery slopes of the Cloghoge valley close at hand.

At the valley floor cross one bridge and just before a second, turn right up a side track, parallel to the Cloghoge Brook. Tackle Fancy (? *Fuinnse*, Ash Tree: 595m/1,956ft) from anywhere along here, through bracken and rough heather and with the occasional stretch of path obligingly leading in the right direction.

The cliffs of Fancy belie its rather dull top, a heather plateau stretching away to the northwest, but commanding magnificent middle distance views, prominent among which is the great bulk of Djouce, now to be tackled. To do so take a path running north from the summit heading towards a major bridge at 154 095 on the R759, crossing on the way the delightful upper Cloghoge River where there are excellent spots for a leisurely snack.

Cross the R759 at the major bridge and walk upstream along the river which the bridge spans through a desolate wet moorland towards the Coffin Stone, a prominent heap of stones crowned by the massive boulder which gives the whole assembly its highly appropriate name.

The ascent to Djouce is easy navigationally, whatever about corporeally: go south uphill and then pick up the line of fence posts and follow it right to the semi-plateau on which Djouce (725m/2,385ft) stands. The summit is marked by three large out-crops of schist and a trig. point so it is unmistakable and the views predictably magnificent.

The descent is along its southern spur towards White Hill from which elevated route the Barnacullian ridge to the west, linking the second and third highest peaks in Wicklow, may be seen to perfection.

On this descent you will pick up the Wicklow Way, which you follow going south for the rest of the route. This route offers excellent views, best of all when the cliffs of Fancy, with Lough Tay tucked in beneath them, are revealed suddenly and dramatically.

The last stretch is through mixed forest and cleared land. This would involve complicated directions were it not for the necessarily frequent Wicklow Way markers. Once on the road, the R759 again, turn left and walk downhill for about 1km/0.6 miles to the start.

Distance: 13.5km/8.5miles. Ascent 720m/2,400ft. Walking time: 5½ hours.

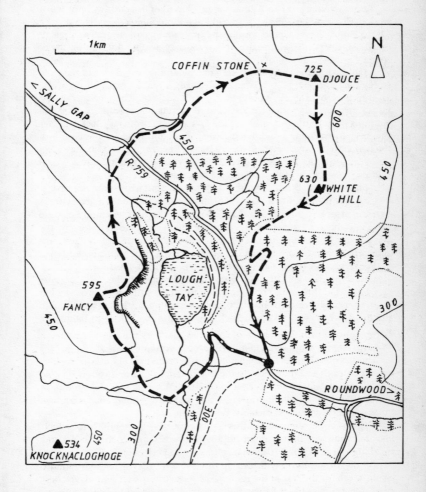

Reference OS Maps: Wicklow District (1:63,360) or Sheet 56 (1:50,000).

12. BALLINRUSH GATES TO LOUGH DAN

Lovely scenery, an undemanding walk, secluded places to picnic and swim — just the formula to transform a sultry summer day into something memorable. This short walk, demanding little effort, takes in some of the best of Wicklow's scenery.

Take the N11 by car to Kilmacanoge, 5km/3miles south of Bray. Turn right here onto the R755 and turn right again onto the R759 after a further 11km/7miles. Drive uphill for 3.2km/2miles and park near the gateway on the left marked 'Ballinrush'. This walk may also be done using the St Kevin's bus.

Take the track at the Ballinrush gateway all the way down to the two-storey house at Lough Dan 3km/2miles away. This is a really lovely walk, an interplay of rugged mountain, valley and lake. The steady descent means that the shoulders of the nearer mountains eventually hide the summits — but little matter. Near the lake private property blocks further progress. Turn right here down a narrow path and head for the river and the two-storey house where there are places to eat and rest (you may have difficulty justifying the latter to yourself). If you potter round a little you'll find places to swim, but avoid private property.

Time to return. Start back the way you came but just before the first — let's dignify it — 'summer residence' on the right, turn onto a grassy track heading steeply upwards (you will soon note that the seemingly meagre drop on the outward journey is more than compensated for by the comparatively horrendous rise on the return). At the ruin on the left turn right uphill beside forest, turn left onto a track a little way up and when you observe, half-right, a gate set high on the horizon, head for it.

Cross the gate and turn left with forest directly on the left. Continue straight ahead through a short stretch of forest on a firebreak, crossing left over a fence where convenient, to join an inviting track. Turn right onto this track which will take you back close to the road close to Ballinrush gates.

Distance: 6.5km/4miles. Ascent: 210m/700ft. Walking time: 2½ hours.

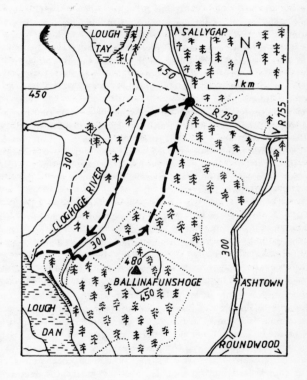

Reference OS Maps: Wicklow District (1:63,360) or Sheet 56 (1:50,000).

13. SCARR AND KNOCKNACLOGHOGE FROM OLDBRIDGE

Scarr is at the centre of one of the most shapely mountain areas in Wicklow. Itself a grassy up-and-down ridge running north and south, it sends three broad grassy spurs out towards the east and a delightful rocky hummocky ridge, Kanturk Mountain, running in a wide crescent towards the north. North of Kanturk is the narrow flat trough of the Inchavore River and northwards again looms rocky Knocknacloghoge, somewhat overshadowed by its higher southern neighbour. Add to this the sylvan valley of the Cloghoge River and the result is one of the most delightful walking areas in the Wicklow Mountains.

This is a route which may be conveniently undertaken by St Kevin's bus to Roundwood. Check times for the return before you start! By car drive to Roundwood on the R755, follow signs here towards Lough Dan and park in a grassy patch on the left at Oldbridge (158 017) 4.2km/2.5miles from Roundwood.

From Oldbridge walk north for a few minutes to the first turn on the left, a stony track. Follow it for about 1km/0.5miles to a forestry plantation and then turn right and follow the forest's edge, keeping it on your left, to a very wide firebreak (no need to do what I once did in gross and painful ignorance: crawl through the dense forest hereabouts on my tummy). Once out of forest and on the northmost of the three spurs the climb to Scarr is straightforward and steady.

The summit of Scarr (*sceir* or *scor*, Sharp Rock: 641m/2,108ft) is un-cairned but the series of little grassy mounds forming the top is unmistakable. The views of the Barnacullian ridge to the west are particularly fine, especially after rain when the tributaries of the Glenmacnass River cascade down the steep-sided slopes into the glen below.

From the top of Scarr, walk northwest to cross a rickety fence leading to a broad ridge. If you need reassurance that you are on course you may come across a roughly hewn pillar standing on this shoulder. Continue northwards to the area of hummocks, Kanturk, already described. The problem now is to find the firebreak which runs directly down to the copse on the Inchavore River at 133 047. If you can find a large egg-shaped erratic boulder on the ridge, a compass bearing of 22° will take you to the top of the firebreak — otherwise it's trial and, I hope, not too much error.

The copse is a delightful spot. The shady oaks and the deep pools of the stream make an ideal place for a well-deserved rest. After that let's hope you have sufficient energy to tackle Knocknacloghoge. Cross the river at the copse and, keeping the forest fence on the left, head towards the summit. Knocknacloghoge (*cloghog*, Stony Land; 534m/1,754ft) has a small neat cairn set on a jagged rocky summit. The views of Lough Dan and back to Scarr are particularly fine.

North of Knocknacloghoge, head directly for the Cloghoge Brook and once on the far side walk downstream. If the weather is hot, leave time to bathe at a delectable spot further down the brook. A little below this pool and still on the left bank pick up a track, take it to the main track, turn left and head up to the R759 at Pier Gates. This involves a punishing 180m/600ft climb, not exactly an inviting prospect towards the end of the day.

From Pier Gates follow Route 14 and the Wicklow Way back to Oldbridge.

Distance: 19km/12miles. Ascent: 960m/3,200ft. Walking time: 7½ hours.

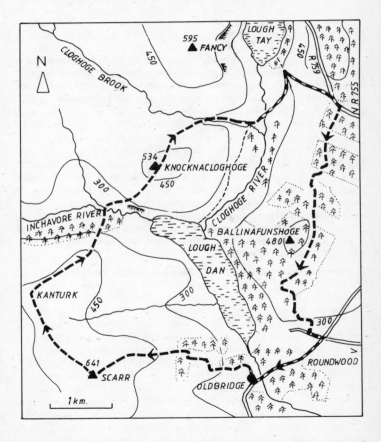

Reference OS Maps: Wicklow District (1:63,360) or Sheet 56 (1:50,000).

14. EASY CIRCUIT OF LOUGH DAN

If you want an easy day in lovely surroundings without climbing any mountains you could do worse, in truth you could hardly do better, than take this variation on Walk 13 along the western end of Lough Dan and finish as in Walk 13 on the Wicklow Way. A beautiful walk.

Transport is as in Walk 13.

From Oldbridge walk northeast along tarmac for about 1.5km/1mile, to where the road swings left after a bridge and deteriorates to gravel. Cross a gate right opposite 'Carrigeen Lodge' and follow a wisp, but an improving wisp, of a path parallel to the shore below on the right. Turn right where the path joins a track and continue onwards, a tiny flat grassy plain on the right with the rocky cliffs of Knocknacloghoge beyond it, to the oak copse further upstream.

Cross the river here and head downstream to the two-storey house at the outlet of the Cloghoge River into Lough Dan. The valley traversed beyond the house must be one of the loveliest in Wicklow: Knocknacloghoge rising on the left, wooded Sleamaine on the right and the neat fields of the glen between. The track up the valley crosses the river and climbs up steeply past the Luggala Entrance Lodge to the R759 at Pier Gates. By the time you read this, there may be an Interpretive Centre and carpark there.

Turn right onto the R759 and walk 200m/180yds or so down the road to a Wicklow Way marker leading into forest. The next 4km/2.5miles is along the Way on the eastern flank of the Sleamaine-Ballinafunshoge ridge, a high-level (or perhaps better described as 'high but level') route along forest tracks through a pleasant mixture of mature and new forest and heathery moorland. Close to Lake Park, the Way descends southeast between fields to tarmac. Turn right here and walk the 1.5km/1mile back to the car at Oldbridge or walk straight ahead (still on tarmac) to Round-wood, 2.5km/1.5miles away.

Distance: 16km/10 miles. Ascent: 270m/900ft. Walking time: 5 hours.

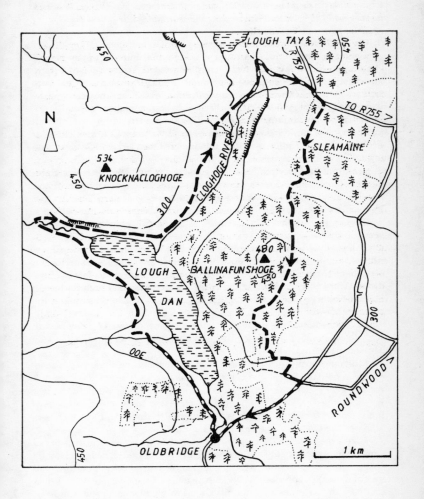

Reference OS Maps: Wicklow District (1:63,360) or Sheet 56 (1:50,000).

15. CIRCUIT OF GLENBRIDE

Wicklow is seen here in its quintessence. Bleak rolling moorland, decaying and extant peat hags and, mercifully and unusually, an unforested terrain all make for a landscape which is Wicklow at what is normally considered its purest and most typical. Nonetheless, this is not all gentle slopes. The climb of Mullaghcleevaun, Wicklow's second highest mountain, gives a focus and goal to the day's endeavours.

To get to the start of this route you are going to have to pay careful attention to the car's milometer. Turn onto the R756 from the N81 11km/7miles south of Blessington. After another 11km/7miles turn left onto tarmac. Turn right after 1.6km/1 mile. Park carefully near the bridge at the hamlet of Glenbride (037 043) another 1.6km/1 mile further on.

Alternatively you might take the R758, forking left (ignore the left turn just before the fork) 1.3km/0.8miles beyond Valleymount, fork left after another 1.8km/1.1miles, and turn left after another 2.7km/1.7miles parking at Glenbride as above.

From the bridge walk back along the road, cross the first gate right, into the forest, walk directly upwards and cross the forest's upper fence. Head uphill through heather and open pathless moorland to Silsean (*Soillsean*, Place of Lights: 698m/2,296ft). 'Place of lights' perhaps, but not much to identify the summit, a plateau of wet bogland interspersed with an occasional shallow lakelet.

The shallow gap towards Moanbane is a relatively good place for a rest and food — shelter is even more scarce further on. The short rise to Moanbane (*Moin Bhan*, White Bog; 703m/2,313ft) is a mirror image of the descent from Silsean. In bad visibility the walker unfamiliar with the terrain might be forgiven for supposing that he is back at Silsean, so similar is the summit plateau.

Beyond Moanbane is Billy Byrne's Gap, a region of austere wet windswept bogland which yields in turn to steep, drier ground towards Mullaghcleevaun itself.

Mullaghcleevaun (*Mullach Cliabhain*, Summit of the Basket i.e. corrie: 847m/2,788ft) stands at the centre of peaks and offers good views but, mainly because of the gentle slopes around, not as good as its height would suggest. Near the summit cairn and close to the steep dip sweeping down to Cleevaun Lough is a memorial to three An Oige members who perished in a boating tragedy in the fifties.

Take especial care on the descent from Mullaghcleevaun: two broad similar spurs run roughly south, one slightly east of south, the other slightly west. Remember, the spur west of south is the correct one. An error could be unfortunate! Approaching the headwaters of the Glasnagollum Brook on this spur is a strange area of black mud formed by collapsed peat hags, an area whose weirdness is accentuated if cloud clings to the hills. Not a place to linger over.

The Glasnagollum Brook leads down towards the bottom of Glenbride where Hobson's Choice is between wet feet and weary legs: a judicious detour right will lead to a somewhat drier traverse. Once on the opposite bank, turn left and you will shortly pick up a track leading back to the car.

Distance: 12km/7.5miles. Ascent: 630m/2,100ft. Walking time: 4½ hours.

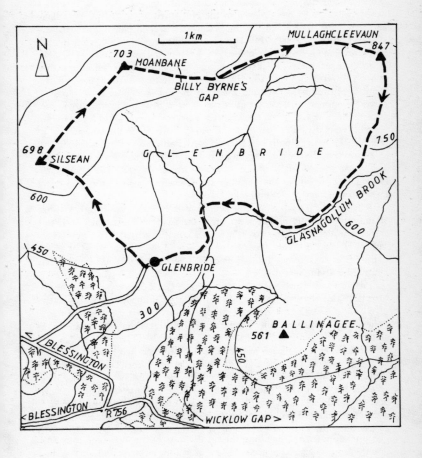

Reference OS Maps: Wicklow District (1:63,360) or Sheet 56 (1:50,000).

16. LUGNAGUN, SORREL AND BLACK HILL

The broad expanse of Pollaphuca Reservoir is never far away on this walk, white against blue reflecting scudding clouds, or leaden grey surfaces producing an effect of mourning heightened by the steady drizzle of the 'soft' day. The mountains adjoining the reservoir are gently sloped and therefore wet but afforestation has not yet laid its monotonous green carpet on a landscape which still faithfully reflects the season's changes.

By car drive to Blessington on the N81, turn left (east) in the village and drive a further 3.5km/2.2miles towards Lackan parking at a cul-de-sac road on the left (993 024). The route might possibly be done using the Ballyknockan version of the 65 bus route but check times.

Walk up the cul-de-sac road taking the forest track left at the fork about 1km/0.6miles up. After it bends sharply to the right take one of a number of firebreaks running uphill on the left — choose a clear one — across two forest tracks and onto open ground near the top of Lugnagun, a nebulous peak which may be ignored. Turn right once out of forest to face Sorrel (*Samhradh*, Hill of Summer?: 599m/1,976ft) the large bare mound to the east, following a path and later an earth bank towards the summit.

Sorrel has a large cairn standing on a plateau of strewn granite rocks. The views towards Pollaphuca Reservoir are excellent; Mullaghcleevaun towers formidably to the south with Black Hill rising more modestly closer to hand across Ballynultagh Gap.

It is Black Hill which is the next goal. Descend over rough heather southwards to Ballynultagh Gap, cross the road at the carpark and start the ascent along the bog road, a road shamefully disfigured by several dumps. The road expires near the summit and the walker must carry on to the featureless rounded top of Black Hill (602m/1,984ft), a summit bereft of any identifying features.

Push on south towards the headwaters of Cock Brook and at the brook turn right downstream to reach a lateral wall. Climb right, parallel to the wall and, close to a ruin near the brook, you will meet the end of a track. Follow it mostly downhill to tarmac at the Lackan-Ballyknockan (lakeshore) road.

Turn left here, walk for nearly 1km/0.5miles and just beyond a bridge take a grassy path on the right down to the reservoir. Turn right at the shore and walk along it to Lackan where there is easy — and legal — access back to tarmac. The lakeshore walk makes for slow going, with boulders and rocks to negotiate and a deal of wet sand and gravel to sink into. Nonetheless it is worth taking this detour for the pleasant views across the waters to the hills beyond. At Lackan continue on tarmac to the car.

Distance: 18km/11miles. Ascent: 520m/1,700ft. Walking time: 6 hours.

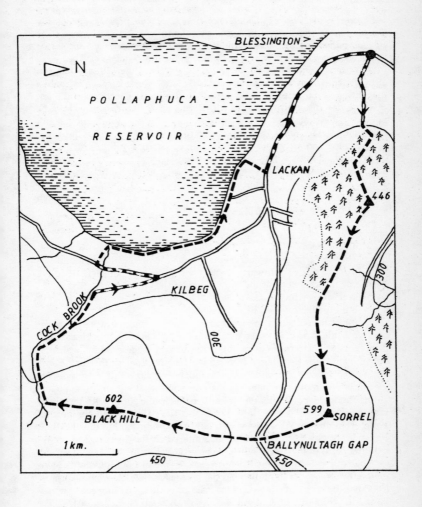

Reference OS Maps: Wicklow District (1:63,360) or Sheet 56 (1:50,000).

49

17. MULLAGHCLEEVAUN AND TONELAGEE

*The second and third highest mountains in Wicklow, Mullaghcleevaun
and Tonelagee, are linked by a broad undulating ridge never dipping
below 600m/2,000ft, riven in some parts by deeply fissured bogland
and covered in other parts by flat areas of sticky black mud. Indeed the only really
firm terrain on this walk is the short grass north and east of Tonelagee. The
panorama around it and particularly down onto the steep corrie of heart-shaped
Lough Ouler is magnificent and forms a fitting climax to the day's walk.*

Park in the small carpark on the right (west) of the Military Road at
101 050 about 9km/5.5miles south of Sally Gap. There is space for only a
few cars here but more can be parked in the forest entrance on the left
(east), a few hundred metres north. If you have two cars, one may be
parked in Glenmacnass carpark on the right, nearly 3km/2miles south
along the Military Road, thus avoiding a road walk at the end of the day.

From the carpark climb the right side of Carrigshouk (571m/1,877ft)
on an intermittent path, avoiding the steep slabs of the direct approach.
The summit of Carrigshouk may be bypassed and Mullaghcleevaun East
Top tackled directly over featureless terrain. East Top (795m/2,609ft) has a
small cairn and a more impressive heap of boulders which looks as though
it is artfully arranged to form a modern sculpture. Beyond the East Top a
sea of oozy bog confronts the walker intent on a direct approach; a prudent
tack to starboard (right) is advisable.

Mullaghcleevaun (847m/2,788ft) is described under Walk 15; enough
to say that the trig. pillar and memorial plaque are sufficient identification. Take the ridge southwards (with the slightest hint of east) along the
Barnacullian ridge here, at the headwaters of the Glenmacnass River, rent
by deep fissures which make for tortuous progress. If you wish to avoid
sticky mud further on keep to the east of the ridge.

South of Barnacullian the ground is better — rough grass and moorland. A gentle drop is followed by a distinct rise to Stoney Top. Head south
from Stoney Top to confront the steep rise to Tonelagee close by, watching
out, in cloud, for the grassy cliffs above Lough Ouler to the east. Tonelagee (*Toin le gaoth*, Backside to the Wind: 817m/2,686ft) is an impressive
viewpoint, far more commanding than the somewhat higher Mullaghcleevaun. The waters of Turlough Hill are visible to the south with the entire
Lugnaquilla massif to its right. Scarr and the other mountains around
Lough Dan dominate the east with a bumpy skyline. Add to this the great
corrie of Lough Ouler, soon to be encountered on the descent, and the remaining pains of the ascent will soon be forgotten.

The rock-strewn descent along the south side of Lough Ouler is navigationally straightforward. Beyond the lake featureless moorland warrants
a compass bearing directly to Glenmacnass carpark. To avoid wet feet it may
be worth while diverting about 70m/yds upstream of the carpark where
there are natural stepping stones. From the carpark walk uphill to the car
(if you have to).

Assuming two cars:
Distance: 13.5km/8.5miles. Ascent: 700 m/2,300ft. Walking time: 5½ hours.

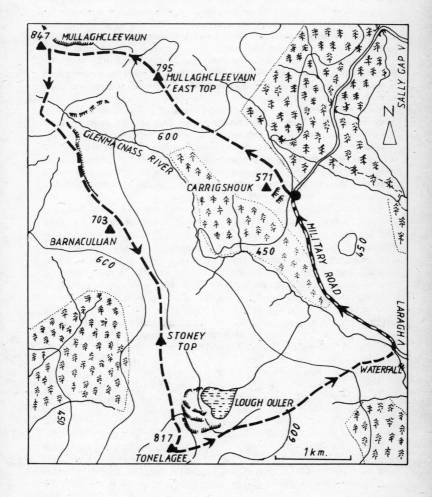

Reference OS Maps: Wicklow District (1:63,360) or Sheet 56 (1:50,000).

18. FAIR MOUNTAIN AND LOUGH FIRRIB

The region south of the Wicklow Gap road (the R756) is a high, wide desolate moorland without notable landmarks. It is therefore an ideal area for the aspiring navigator to try out his skills, indeed not only to try them out but have them rigorously examined. The reward for success is the satisfaction of finding one's way between small and secluded features on a bleak moorland. The penalty for failure might be hours of tiring trudging over endless peat hags — but let's not even think about that!

Car only. Turn onto the R756 from the N81 11km/7miles south of Blessington. Drive a further 12km/7.7miles, turning right onto a side road here. (Watch out carefully for it!) Drive 0.5km/0.3miles further and park near the bridge (at 033 020).

Take the forest track past the forest bar and follow it and, alas, the huge Turlough Hill electricity pylons, to the first hairpin bend, a right. Here look out carefully on the left for a narrow but clear path heading into forest. After about 5 minutes walking it peters out, to be replaced by a helpful firebreak running upwards on the right. A few anxious paces later the walker emerges between mature forest and saplings and sees a little way up a rocky mound, probably unique in this area and therefore an assurance of the correct path.

Cross the fence just beyond the boulders and turn left (east). With the fence as a guide you can now relax from navigational concerns for a while and admire the scenery, primarily north towards Tonelagee across the Wicklow Gap. As you advance, Fair Mountain, huge boulders along its flank, increasingly dominates the way ahead until, at a major stream flowing between scattered conifers, a choice must be made between a frontal assault up a steep rock-strewn slope or the subtler approach of walking upstream a little and tackling the mountain from there.

The views from the summit of Fair Mountain (569m/1,867ft) are little better than those from lower down, Tonelagee still the major natural feature. What is new is a major manmade feature, the ramparts of the top reservoir of Turlough Hill. And it is on these ramparts that attention must now focus. Head southeast from Fair Mountain, pick up a short stretch of tarmac near the reservoir and, at the level ground above, face Lough Firrib.

Lough Firrib is tiny: snugly hidden among undulating moorland it is far from easy to find. You may be lucky and pick up a trench or a set of bootprints (hardly a path) which runs to the lough or you may choose self-reliance and the compass. Either way Lough Firrib is a good place to rest and eat, and to prepare for the next stage, the leg to Art's Cross.

Art's Cross (038 990) is, slightly surprisingly, actually a wooden cross set above steep ground overlooking Glenreemore. On clear days, when you don't need it for navigation, it is visible for miles; on bad days, when you do, you won't see it till you bump against it. Such are the trials of the hill walker.

From Art's Cross you can drop into Glenreemore but if you wish to retain wide views, keep high by heading over open ground into the vee formed by the Glenreemore and Asbawn Brooks, cross right over the former and walk downstream through wet ground between two forests to the electricity pylons at the 'cul' of a cul-de-sac road.

From here to the start it is 'simply' a matter of continuing to follow the Glenreemore Brook downstream to its junction with the Kings River and then following the Kings upstream. 'Simple' navigationally but some tough wet terrain makes for slow progress, in particular at the junction where young conifers (don't tread on them!) are planted. After this, underfoot conditions gradually improve and you can enjoy a pleasant riverside walk, a walk which may be enhanced by the sight of a heron fishing among the boulders of the river.

Distance: 13.5km/8.5miles. Ascent 480m/1,600ft. Walking time: 4½ hours.

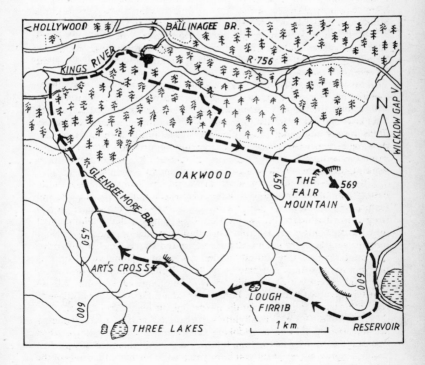

Reference OS Maps: Wicklow District (1:63,360) or Sheet 56 (1:50,000).

19. THREE LAKES AND ART'S CROSS

This is an area where the next peat hag to be surmounted, or the nearest stretch of dull rolling moorland to be trudged, limits visibility to a few soggy square yards. Nevertheless the sudden unexpected glimpses of Moanbane or Tonelagee looming across the Wicklow Gap and the satisfaction of finding the next insignificant landmark in a well-nigh featureless area make this walk rewarding. Don't attempt it in bad visibility unless you are very sure of your navigational skills!

Car only. Turn onto the R756 from the N81 11km/7miles south of Blessington. Drive for a further 8km/5miles to Granabeg (004 021), a hamlet whose most notable feature is the telephone kiosk on the right (south) of the road.

Starting close to the kiosk, walk south down a path through fields to the Kings River, cross it by a metal bridge and ascend the south bank to tarmac. Note where you reached the road — you will need this information for the return. Cross the road diagonally left to pass through a gate. Walk straight uphill with a band of forest on each side to the fence which provides a common boundary to these bands. Say farewell to civilisation and prepare for a time of trouble!

From here to Lough Firrib your route is punctuated by a series of obscure landmarks not *all* of which you need find though it will certainly add to your peace of mind if you do. Round Hill (511m/1,677ft) at 003 995 is a gently sloping spur 'distinguished by' a few stones, an unusual feature in an area of bogland. Then follows the boundary ditch climbing Table Mountain at about 005 979, Three Lakes (in spite of the name there are only two), the wooden Art's Cross at 038 990 and finally Lough Firrib. A not very prominent series of goals set in ubiquitous moorland to save you (literally) from a sticky end.

From Lough Firrib you can take the high road over the spur to the north or the low road down into Glenreemore, depending on the day and your inclination. Let's assume a descent into Glenreemore (the high route is described in Walk 18). Head directly northwest over fairly steep ground into a delightful pocket at the head-waters of the Glenreemore Brook. (Look out among the rocky slabs on the left for the plaque to Art O'Neill.) Wander down the right bank, past the incoming tributary of the Asbawn Brook and into a wide gap between two plantations (this gap is not indicated on the maps). Cross the bridge just beyond the power lines and turn left onto tarmac. A little over 1.5km/1mile west on tarmac, turn right for the metal bridge and the car.

Distance: 14.5km/9miles. Ascent : 440m/1,450ft. Walking time: 5 hours.

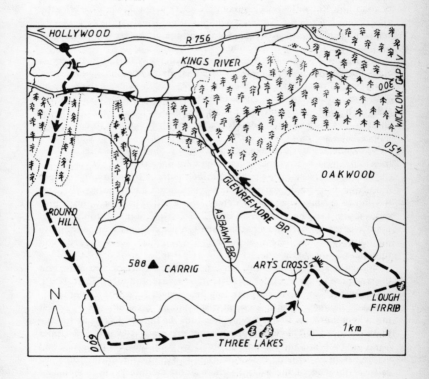

Reference OS Maps: Wicklow District (1:63,360) or Sheet 56 (1:50,000).

20. THE SPINK AND THE DERRYBAWN RIDGE

The wooded Spink rears impressively over the eastern end of the Upper Lake at Glendalough and runs from there along its southern shore in a line of sheer cliffs occasionally indented by rocky bluffs. After an impressive start along the Spink the route takes us to grassy, gently sloped Mullacor and down narrow Derrybawn, a rib of metamorphic rock and the finest ridge in Wicklow. A short but memorable walk.

Car to the upper carpark, Glendalough (111 964) about 1.5km/1mile beyond the Royal Hotel Glendalough. Or take St Kevin's bus to the Glendalough terminus. Travellers by bus should walk into the cemetery containing the Round Tower, cross the bridge at the far end, turn right and walk the 1.5km/1mile or so to the start proper.

Climb up the steps by the foaming Pollanass Waterfall to the forest track and at the multiple junction turn sharply right uphill onto a track signposted 'Prezen Rock'. At the first bend — a left — cross the fence on your right, using the stile, and climb steeply upwards to the top of the Spink. The first sight from the crest of the Spink is breath-taking — if the climb to this lofty vantage point leaves you with any breath to take — the Upper Lake seemingly at your feet, the great cliffs south of Camaderry half-left, and the undulating crest of the Spink reaching towards the high hills to the west — it's a marvellous panorama.

Follow the crest of the Spink parallel to the Upper Lake on a very muddy path, a small matter in such magnificent surroundings. Beyond the end of the lake the scenery deteriorates a little but a forest track provides easier walking, though all uphill. (To dispel niggling doubts about your location you should note that the Ordnance Survey maps simplify the boundary of the forest on the left — it is actually very ragged. Nor, understandably, do they depict the huge clear-felled areas of forest.)

Near the saddle point between Lugduff and Mullacor you must quit the track and climb Mullacor (*Mullach mhor*, Great Summit: 657m/2,179ft), a rounded grassy peak commanding fine views especially towards the Lugnaquilla massif. On the descent east keep the forest in view on the left but where it swings sharply away, head for the bumpy Derrybawn ridge to the northeast. The views along here, especially towards the Upper Lake, are excellent and the terrain, a narrow path, much of it on rock and sloping sharply away on both sides, allows a confident striding out. The cairn at the end of the ridge — there is no definite peak — signals a descent over heather into forest. The point to aim for is the shallow vee formed by the forest at 125 963. Plunge into forest here, cross one track and turn left on the second. Fork first right, joining the Wicklow Way and then first right again leaving the Way, a sharp turn just before a bridge. This takes you down to the valley floor where a left takes you to the car and a right to the bus.

While you are at Glendalough, it would be a pity (if you don't already know them) not to visit the monastic ruins below the Lower Lake. The Interpretive Centre at the Lower Carpark is also well worth a visit.

Distance: 13km/8miles. Ascent: 510m/1,700ft. Walking time: 4½ hours.

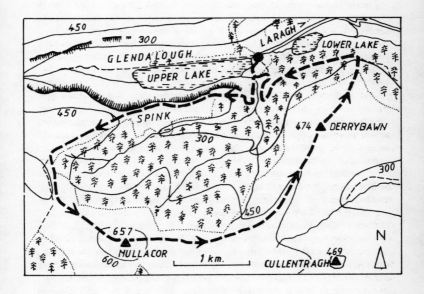

Reference OS Maps: Wicklow District (1:63,360) or Sheet 56 (1:50,000).

21. GLENEALO, TURLOUGH HILL AND CAMADERRY

The view west up the Upper Lake Glendalough towards Glenealo is magnificent, seen by countless thousands of day trippers annually and captured on hundreds of photos and drawings. But what about the view from Glenealo east towards Glendalough? It is equally good (probably better) but is seen and enjoyed only by the hardy souls who ascend the zig-zags terminating the western end of Glendalough. Add to this Camaderry, the great wedge of mountain lying between Glendalough and Glendasan, and the ingredients are those of a most enjoyable walk.

Start at the upper carpark, Glendalough (111 964). Directions are given under Walk 20.

From the carpark join the throngs (on Sundays anyway) strolling along the shores of the Upper Lake. Beyond its end, thread a way through the old mine workings. While these are not a thing of beauty and certainly promise to be an eyesore forever, they are interesting geologically. They stand on a metamorphic zone between the granite further west and the ancient Ordovician strata to the east which were thrust aside by the up-swelling granite. Similar workings occur in Glendasan and Glenmalure, all three along this zone.

Ascending the zig-zags you will find some excellent resting and swimming places along the river on the left; they are especially good higher up. (On hot days better take a solemn vow before you stop that you won't abort the walk!) The scenery is not quite so good on the fairly level ground in Glenealo and you can concentrate on pleasant, though wet, walking along the left (true) bank of the river.

Continue up the valley taking the main stream rather than tributaries and at the soggy headwaters climb the remaining distance to the level ground between tiny Lough Firrib and the gigantic sloping sides of Turlough Hill Reservoir. Thanking your lucky stars that you have to find the latter rather than the former, walk round the southern perimeter fence of the reservoir, negotiate the peat hags beyond and ascend Camaderry (*Ceim a' doire*, Pass of the Oakwood: 698m/2,296ft) which has a rather flat top thus making the cairn particularly useful. There is a lower second peak of Camaderry to the southeast, after which a good path gives easy walking right down the spur between Glendasan on the left and Glendalough on the right, a long easy descent with lovely views.

You can cut the walk short by descending a steep path right to the upper carpark, but if you have the time why should you? Instead continue down the spur, pick up a forest track near the end, turn right onto it and it will guide you back on a boomerang's progress high above the shore of the Lower Lake and then gently to earth near the eastern end of the Upper Lake to end what should have been an enjoyable day.

Distance: 14.5km/9miles. Ascent: 600m/2,000ft. Walking time: 5 hours.

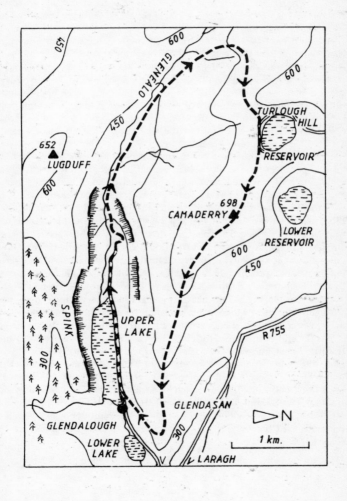

LUGDUFF

652

GLENEALO

600

450

450

600

600

TURLOUGH HILL

RESERVOIR

698

CAMADERRY

LOWER RESERVOIR

600

450

SPINK

300

UPPER LAKE

R 755

GLENDASAN

N

1 km.

GLENDALOUGH

LOWER LAKE

300

LARAGH

Reference OS Maps: Wicklow District (1:63,360) or Sheet 56 (1:50,000).

22. CARRIGLINNEEN AND MULLACOR

Carriglinneen is a small but craggy peak and the initial climb from its south side is stiff but satisfying. You next cross the Military Road where the peaks are rounded and a trifle bland but give extensive panoramas. The walk ends with a section of the Wicklow Way offering excellent views down into Glenmalure.

By car drive 1.4km/0.9miles south of Laragh on the R755, turning right sharply uphill here for Glenmalure. Drive on for another 7km/4.5miles to Drumgoff crossroads (107 909), turn left and park immediately on the right.

From the crossroads walk southeast along the road, looking for a suitable place within 500m/550yds to cross left onto rough open ground (the exact point is immaterial but avoid enclosed fields). The climb from here to the summit of Carriglinneen (? *carraig glinnin*, Rock of the Little Glen: 455m/1,507ft) is steep, but the rocky crags hereabouts are easily avoided, or, if you prefer it, easily climbed.

The summit is indistinct but the next stretch northeast along the high ground parallel to the Military Road is clear enough. Follow a path which widens to a narrow track, and which eventually joins a wide track heading to the highest point on tarmac between Laragh and Glenmalure.

Cross the road (the appropriately located memorial to the cyclist Shay Elliot near the top of the hill is worth the slight detour) and take the forest road on the other side. The rule from here on as far as Mullacor is to keep straight on regardless: walk (in turn) on a good track, a narrow track, a path with an accompanying ditch and finally open pathless terrain, on the way bypassing Cullentragh. Beyond it watch out on the right for the Derrybawn ridge bumping northwards on its rocky route towards Glendalough.

Mullacor (657m/2,179ft) has an excellent location for long views and the steep drop to be walked west beyond it renders it unmistakable if only in retrospect — its imminence is not particularly evident from the southeast.

At the end of this drop, turn left along a series of white posts heading towards forest, and near the forest pick up a conventional Wicklow Way post. The Way can now be followed right back to the start. Running first parallel to the forest, it then plunges down through it , wavers indecisively on a track and on a lovely stretch of secluded path, and belatedly but resolutely heads straight back southeast above the valley floor, swings left into the side valley containing the Military Road and deposits the walker on tarmac at Coolalingo Bridge. Turn right here and walk the short distance to Drumgoff.

Distance: 14.5km/9miles. Ascent: 610m/2,000ft. Walking time: 5 hours.

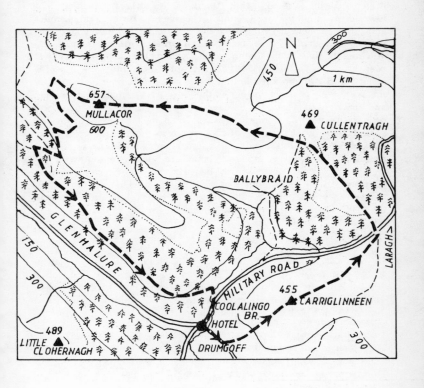

Reference OS Maps: Wicklow District (1:63,360) or Sheet 56 (1:50,000).

23. GLENMALURE, THE FRAUGHAN ROCK GLEN AND LUGNAQUILLA

Probably the most rewarding approach to Lugnaquilla is from Baravore at the head of Glenmalure. A short but steep ascent via a series of tiny valleys culminates in Wicklow's only 900m/3,000ft summit, and is followed by a high-level easy stroll with stunning views in all directions. A lovely walk.

Car only though this walk may also be done from Glenmalure youth hostel. Take the R755 for 1.4km/0.9miles south of Laragh turning right here steeply uphill towards Glenmalure. Drive for a further 7km/4.5miles and turn right here at Drumgoff at the crossroads. Park in the large car-park at the head of the valley (at 068 941) a further 5km/3miles on.

Cross the river by the footbridge and walk on tarmac upstream to just past the youth hostel. Fork left steeply uphill here and walk upwards along a track through forest until it comes close to the river on the left (at this point there is also a junction in the forest track). Cross the river here and turn right to face up the Fraughan Rock Glen. The scenery from here on is spectacular — and improves as you go on: the far wall of Glenmalure behind, the rugged shoulder of Clohernagh to the left, the great rocky cliffs of Ben Leagh to the right and ahead as you advance the rapids cascading over the steep ground which bounds the glen to the southwest.

Keeping to the narrow path between fence and river to avoid trespassing, walk to the rapids and then climb parallel to them to a second higher valley, this one generally wet and perhaps a little dull. Climbing the easily surmountable rocky wall behind it reveals a third valley, and when you climb the steep grassy slope behind this, the gently sloped terrain above heralds the summit plateau of Lugnaquilla itself.

The view from the immediate area of the great cairn on Lugnaquilla (*Log na Coille*, Hollow of the Cocks; 925m/3,039ft) is dull, a grassy plateau whose pastoral atmosphere is accentuated by grazing sheep. But walk a few yards in any direction and a great panorama is suddenly revealed. The high hills of the range crowd in from all directions: whalebacked Tonelagee and Mullaghcleevaun to the north, Keadeen to the west, the long spur of Clohernagh reaching out to the east, to the southeast the graceful cone of Croaghanmoira, and Mount Leinster, topped by its TV aerial, to the south. A wonderful series of views.

From Lugnaquilla descend on a gentle slope to Clohernagh (*Clocharnach*, Stony Place; 800m/2,623ft), a long stretch with wide spectacular views and excellent underfoot conditions. Just two points about the otherwise easy navigation: firstly if you take a direct bearing from the top of Lug to Clohernagh, be prepared at the start to swerve prudently left to avoid the cliffs of the South Prison, and secondly take care to choose the Clohernagh spur (left) rather than the Carrawaystick spur at the one distinct junction.

From Clohernagh continue east picking up a path overlooking Bendoo cliffs on the left. The aim at the lower end of this path is to find the top of the zig-zag path which runs parallel and to the west of the Carrawaystick Waterfall (these paths do not obligingly join up); a little trial with hopefully not too much error may be necessary. One hint: if you see a slag heap spanning the valley floor below, you will know that the zig-zags emerge onto tarmac a little to the east.

Walk down the zig-zags and through the farmyard at the bottom, taking especial care to leave gates as you found them and in general to act responsibly. Cross a bridge to gain tarmac, turn left and walk less than 3km/2miles to the car.

Distance: 14.5km/9miles. Ascent: 800m/2,600ft. Walking time: 5½ hours.

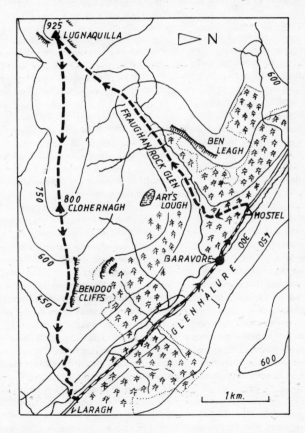

Reference OS Maps: Wicklow District (1:63,360) or Sheet 56 (1:50,000).

24. BALLYBRAID AND MULLACOR

A short walk with some lovely views. A steady rise to Mullacor is followed by a gentle descent along mostly open forest tracks overlooking Glenmalure and the Lugnaquilla massif. The first view of the full extent of Carrawaystick Waterfall is particularly notable.

By car take the R755 for 1.4km/0.9miles south of Laragh. Turn right uphill here and drive for a further 7km/4.5miles to park at the forest entrance on the right (if you have gone nearly as far as Drumgoff cross-roads you have overshot by a few hundred yards).

First you might care to examine Coolalingo Bridge spanning the main road. It's a lovely stone arch — they don't make bridges like that nowadays!

From the forest entrance take the track right (it's the Wicklow Way) but continue straight on where the Way turns left. Follow the track, at first about level, then steeply uphill (don't be tempted by the roads traversing level ground on the right). At the T, turn right, thus heading into Ballybraid valley, the open land of Cullentragh on the right and the wooded south-east spur of Mullacor on the left.

At the hairpin bend at the head of the valley cross right to open ground and continue upward, the forest fence initially on the left, then straight on past the end of the forest to the top of Mullacor. Although only a there-and-back, this detour gives excellent views particularly north and south, the directions of prominent peaks.

Retrace your steps to the corner of the forest and continue down-wards, forest on the left until, after about 15 minutes from this corner, your way is blocked by impenetrable forest. Take the firebreak on the left (when facing this forest and incidentally Carrawaystick Waterfall) and at its end turn right down through a difficult branch-strewn felled area. Emerging gratefully onto a forest road you can study the whole Lugnaquilla massif with the chunky block of Clohernagh to the fore and Carrawaystick cascading vigorously into Glenmalure.

Turn left at this forest road, go right at the fork and turn left at the next decision point (perhaps this would be better described as a 'straight ahead'). This will take you round the southeast spur of Mullacor and high above the side valley carrying the Military Road. Eventually you will discern your car down below on the right, to which you may descend directly — but if you do be especially careful not to tread on saplings.

The more orthodox walker will press on to the right turn 1km/0.6miles ahead and return from there to the car.

Distance: 9km/5.5miles. Ascent: 520m/1,700ft. Walking time: 3½hours.

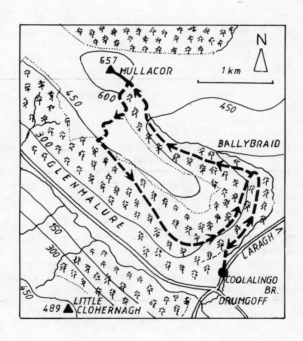

Reference OS Maps: Wicklow District (1:63,360) or Sheet 56 (1:50,000).

65

25. TABLE MOUNTAIN AND THE LUGDUFFS

The start of this walk is lovely but it is an unchanging loveliness. With the heights attained and a stretch of corrugated bogland behind you the delightful ridge of the Lugduffs beckons, offering magnificent views into Glendalough and towards Lugnaquilla. A steep descent into Glenmalure rounds off what should have been a moderately hard but rewarding day.

Car only. Drive to Drumgoff crossroads (no signpost) about 9km/5.5miles from Laragh as described under Walk 23, turn right here and drive to the head of the valley, parking in the large carpark there at 068 491.

From the carpark cross the river and walk upstream on tarmac to the youth hostel. Continue straight ahead on a track beyond it. The gradual ascent of 5km/3miles from carpark to the top of the pass is easy navigationally — simply keep the river close on the right where a choice is to be made. The views, however, though scenic, especially back into Glenmalure, are a trifle unvarying and not helped by recent forestry developments. It may therefore be with some relief that you reach the pass, still on the same track but a track which now threatens to merge forever into the surrounding country.

The pass is the last comfortable place for eating for some time, so after it you may feel up to tackling the next section, a difficult one navigationally. Head north to Table Mountain, a cairn set on a boggy plateau, and then face Three Lakes (there are actually two) which you don't need to reach in good weather but is a useful landmark in bad. The next goal is Conavalla (*Ceann a' bhealaigh*, Head of the Road: 734m/2,421ft), a post set in peat hags, after which a steady descent over bogland ends in the delights of the Lugduff ridge.

The ridge is prefaced by a sharp rise, Lugduff West, and a slight drop followed by another rise ending in Lugduff itself (*Log dubh*, Black Hollow: 652m/2,154ft). In bad visibility it is difficult to gauge exactly how far you have progressed along this ridge, so the bright white quartzite stones just before the summit make identification of this point easy. Keep your fingers crossed for good weather though, for the jagged Spink and later the Upper Lake at Glendalough are just two outstanding features in a panorama running superbly from north through east to south.

Lugduff East is an easy climb over short grass, after which head south-east to descend steeply from the ridge towards Glenmalure, forest close on the left. The last stretch of this descent is through gorse and ferns, the latter if high and therefore fly-infested, being well-nigh intolerable in hot humid summer weather. Once on the road, lick your wounds (if sustained) turn right and walk less than 1.5km/1mile back to the car.

Distance: 16km/10miles. Ascent: 780m/2,600ft. Walking time: 6 hours

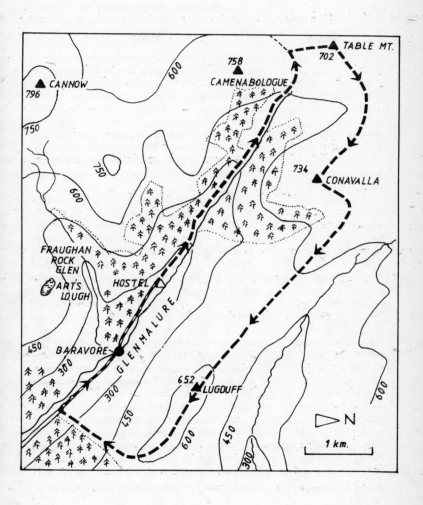

Reference OS Maps: Wicklow District (1:63,360) or Sheet 56 (1:50,000).

26. CARRAWAYSTICK AND CROGHANMOIRA

Croghanmoira, with Great Sugar Loaf, is the nearest approach to the classical pyramid-shaped mountain in Wicklow and though Carrawaystick is merely a spur of Lugnaquilla and not really a distinct peak, under it nestles the delectable Kelly's Lough. It is a pity that a rising tide of monotonous conifers swathes the valleys and threatens the solitude of Kelly's Lough itself. Come before it rises even higher!

Drive to Drumgoff crossroads (107 909) as described under Walk 22.

Walk south past the ruins of the military barracks, turning right after about 300m/330yds, thus following the Wicklow Way. Continue on the Way uphill but where it branches left down into forest continue straight ahead. Turn first right onto another track and continue steadily upwards until the track crosses a bridge spanning the Clohernagh Brook.

New planting hereabouts and the prospect of more makes the next stretch difficult to be precise about. Suffice to say that the aim is to walk upstream along the brook, continue on upwards over the low ridge to the west and head from here downhill to Kelly's Lough, an unusually large corrie lake at a high altitude, and a delightful spot for a rest.

From the eastern end of Kelly's Lough climb the steep slope to its south to Carrawaystick Mountain (*Ceathramhadh istigh*, Inner Quarter: 676m/2,218ft). No need to find its exact top, though if you do find the small cairn perched precariously on a peat hag, count it a bonus. The next target you really must find is an angle in a forest fence southeast of Carrawaystick and about 1.5km/1mile away. The reason for this is to find the wide firebreak beyond it which will take you along the north-western side of Slievemaan, an absolute necessity given the wide tracts of forest all about.

Fifteen minutes walking from the angle in the forest, turn left down a wide grassy firebreak (if you encounter a small cairn on the right you have overshot the firebreak and must return and turn first right). This firebreak ends in a forest track. Turn right onto it and a few minutes later turn left at a point where there is a firebreak on *both* sides. This firebreak leads directly down to the Military Road at the highest point between Drumgoff and Aghavannagh.

Most navigational difficulties now behind, you can face the climb to Croghanmoira with equanimity. Cross the road and follow the path on the opposite side keeping forest on the right till very close to the top. Croghanmoira (?*cruachan maoir*, Hill of the Steward or Overseer: 665m/2,181ft) commands excellent views stretching all the way from Great Sugar Loaf to the Blackstairs. Small wonder then that it was a pivotal point for the triangulation of the country in the original survey in the nineteenth century.

From Croghanmoira walk northeast along the Fananierin ridge, a rocky, narrow rib and one of the best such in the range. Fananierin (?*fan an iarainn*, Slope of the Iron: 427m/1,402ft) at the end of the ridge is not strictly necessary to the route but the views it offers along Glenmalure make it worth the effort.

From here retrace your steps to the lateral stone wall encountered along the ridge and descend half-right to a break in the forest that stretches along the Military Road. Cross the bridge here, walk through the forest to tarmac, turn right and walk the 2.5km/1.5miles to Drumgoff.

Distance: 19km/12miles. Ascent: 780m/2,600ft. Walking time: 6½/7 hours.

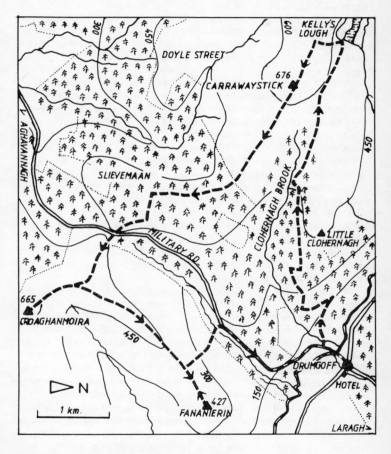

Reference OS Map: Wicklow Way (1:50,000).

27. CIRCUIT OF IMAAL

The circuit of Imaal makes a long and rewarding walk taking in a wide array of high mountain scenery and culminating in Lugnaquilla itself. Whether it is better to do it clockwise or anti-clockwise is a toss-up but anti-clockwise as described below has the advantage of a long scenic descent through magnificent country ahead so that the need to emulate Lot's wife is avoided.

Most of this walk lies within or along the boundary of an Artillery Range. At weekends there is usually no artillery practice, but phone 509845 for information.

Car only. Take the N81 for about 18km/11miles south of Blessington turning left at The Olde Tollhouse for Donard. In Donard take the road east towards the youth hostel (this is straight ahead but the offset cross-roads in Donard may cause brief mystification) and park 2.7km/1.7miles beyond the hostel where the road bends sharply left at Knickeen Ford (986 948). This walk is also suitable for those staying at the youth hostel.

Walk back along the road turning first left a little way down. Ford the river, the Little Slaney, and at the right fork beyond turn left up a track. (Note for law-abiding readers or those of a nervous disposition: this road is in a busy part of the Artillery Range so you may wish, or indeed be forced by military personnel to detour via Seskin (972 935).)

The route is now uphill with scarcely a break all the way to the top of Lugnaquilla. Camarahill (*Camra* ?a sewer(!); 480m/1,567ft) is an insignificant summit after which the rise resumes remorselessly. But be not faint-hearted: magnificent views unfold as you ascend while ahead the huge block of Lugnaquilla beckons, the focus of the day's walk. The last part of this ascent is through a rock-strewn steeply rising area. Keep left here to view the great cliffs of the North Prison.

The summit of Lug is described in Walk 23. For navigational purposes we need only note here that the top is a virtual plateau of short grass topped by a mighty cairn.

The descent, at least initially, requires careful navigation to avoid the cliffs of the North and South Prisons. Descend first northeast and then northwest; then, avoiding the long north-westward spur of Cannow head roughly north keeping to the high ground. As already said this is a marvellous stretch with a lovely panorama of peaks, prominent among which is the great whaleback ridge of Tonelagee. Watch out along here for Art's Lough tucked in below the cliffs north of Clohernagh. Watch out even more to avoid two spurs heading northeast of the correct route which would terminate in grief and painful backtracking above Glenmalure.

The descent over firm ground comes to a sticky end in the peat hags and soggy ground south of Camenabologue (*Ceim na mbulog*, Pass of the Bullocks: 758m/2,495ft) and is followed by a sharp pull-up to its summit, crowned by a large reassuring cairn — reassuring because its magnitude is unique in this area.

Descending north from Camenabologue the next landmark is the pass between it and Table Mountain where an ancient track from Glenmalure crosses west into Imaal. Turn left (west) here downhill following an improving track right down to a forest corner about 1.5km/1mile away. Here an Army waymark, reinforced by a stern Army notice, directs the cowed traveller right downhill, forest on the left. Cross two footbridges further down and pick up a forest track beyond them. (Note that recent felling means that the maps give an impression of much more forest than actually exists.) Follow this track and the Army waymarks back to the car or hostel.

Distance: 17.5km/11miles. Ascent: 850m/2,800 ft. Walking time: 6½ hours.

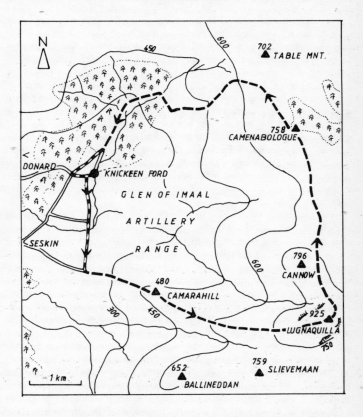

Reference OS Maps: Wicklow District (1:63,360) or Sheet 56 (1:50,000).

28. CHURCH MOUNTAIN AND SUGAR LOAF

From the mountains of the western fringe the eye is inevitably drawn towards the lush plains of Kildare and beyond. The scenery close at hand is generally uninspiring though Lobawn and Sugar Loaf towards the end of the route give fine views over the wide, almost mountain-enclosed basin of the Glen of Imaal. Mostly firm underfoot conditions, interspersed with some very soggy stretches, make for generally easy progress.

By car take the N81 about 18km/11miles south of Blessington and turn left at The Olde Tollhouse. Park in Donard (932 976). The walk may also be adapted to suit those staying at Ballinclea youth hostel. The 65 (Donard) bus serves the village but its infrequency (at the time of writing) does not permit the walk.

From the village walk north on tarmac, cross Intack Bridge and take the first right turn beyond. Walk between high hedges which all too effectively block the view, as far as the last farmhouse (about 1.5km/1mile up) and beyond it head north over a pathless spur to Church, keeping to its left for the views towards the plains.

Church Mountain (544m/1,789ft) is crowned by a truly enormous heap of stones, for which there seems to be no logical explanation. Of yore the locals' speculation was that it was building material for St Kevin's road which ran into Glendalough, a bizarre suggestion given its lofty and inconvenient location. This might be a suitable subject for conjecture as you head over heather to the pass to the southeast and pick up a bog road towards Corriebracks (531m/1,756ft). This road fails to muster enough enthusiasm to climb to the summit and no wonder, for it must be the most unimposing soggy pudding bowl of a mound in the entire Wicklow Mountains.

After Corriebracks descend south over a broad ridge, forest close on the right and further away on the left (these plantations are not marked on most maps) and then climb to the crest of the spur extending west from Lobawn, guided part of the way by a fence on the right. At the crest, where views over Imaal and beyond to bulky Keadeen are suddenly revealed, turn left (east) and following an intermittent ditch marked by occasional stone pillars climb Lobawn (*Loban*, Little Loop; 636m/2,097ft). These impressive views are well sustained on an elevated, almost level, stretch to Sugar Loaf (554m/1,817ft), reached on a reverse L-shaped route from Lobawn.

From Sugar Loaf some attention to navigation is needed. A steep and painful gorse-impeded descent at 280° compass ends in a break in the forest, unexpectedly adorned by a gate. Continuing straight ahead through the gate follow the mature forest on the left to a track. Turn right here, turn left at the T onto a major track, follow this to tarmac close to Snugboro Bridge, turn right and walk the 2.5km/1.5miles into Donard.

Distance: 16km/10miles. Ascent: 700m/2,300ft. Walking time: 6 hours.

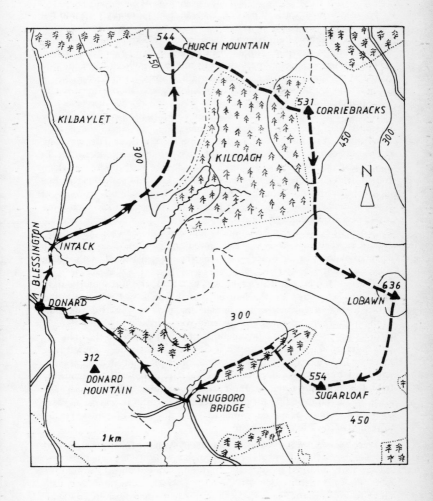

Reference OS Maps: Wicklow District (1:63,360) or Sheet 56 (1:50,000).

73

29. THE BRUSSELSTOWN RING

This is a short (half day) walk over a low outlier of the Wicklow Mountains, a walk which nonetheless gives excellent views. It adds a touch of archaeological interest to exercise mind as well as body.

By far the most difficult part of this walk navigationally is to find the start. Take the N81 to the turn-off for Donard, drive past Ballinclea youth hostel, take the first right beyond it, go straight ahead at the crossroads, fork right to go over the bridge, fork right again just beyond the bridge, go left at the next fork and park carefully at Killybeg (941 901), at the side road 1.9km/1.2miles further on, on the right. Simple, isn't it?

Walk along the side road west from Killybeg and almost immediately your principal target, the Brusselstown Ring, will rise close before you. From the road it appears as a modest green hill with a curious, slightly lop-sided wall encircling the summit mound.

At the T turn right and then left at the hairpin bend. Further along choose any convenient point on the right to climb to the top, 405m/1,329ft high. Near the top you will cross a great double wall of stones, which constitutes a ring fort from the late Stone Age. Unfortunately this ring fort looks much more impressive from nearby Keadeen, but you might console yourself with the thought that Keadeen itself looks much more impressive from here than from *its* top.

Apart from Keadeen, Lugnaquilla and a whole array of other peaks should be visible. There is also a splendid angle on the Glen of Imaal, a scene of almost bucolic peace — except when it is shattered by thudding rocket fire in the Army range.

The next target is Spinan's Hill. A slight drop with forest on the right and a rocky outcrop on the left, beyond which is wet moorland, and you're there — a featureless hill commanding good views across the plains to the west. From Spinan's Hill descend west across a field to a derelict farmhouse which forms a convenient point at which to reach the road.

On the road turn left and walk to Spinan's crossroads. Turn left here and then fork first right. This takes you through pleasant agricultural land enhanced by scattered deciduous trees and then onward by a muddy track through State forest on the northern shoulder of Kilranelagh Hill. Over the hill take the first turn left to regain agricultural land on a grassy track in a country of glacial hummocks and ill-drained hollows. Finally turn right at the T to reach the car.

Distance: 9km/5.5miles. Ascent: 210m/700ft. Walking time: 3 hours.

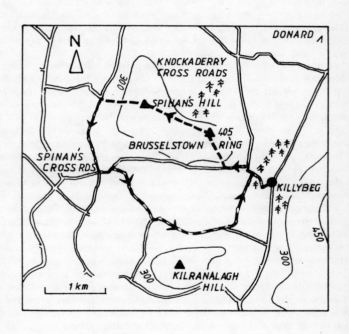

Reference OS Map: Sheet 16 (1:126,720).

30. SLIEVEMAAN AND KEADEEN

Keadeen, the most westerly of all Wicklow's mountains and thus commanding good views west over the plains, is separated from its neighbours to the east by a narrow strip of low ground. You can climb it on its own; however, to make a full day it is desirable to add Slievemaan, an outlier of Lugnaquilla itself. You can climb Slievemaan on its own also! So three walks can be organised with a little adaptation from this one route description.

By car take the N81 to the turn for Donard 18km/11miles south of Blessington. Turn left here, go through Donard to Ballinclea youth hostel and turn first right after it. Continue straight ahead for 2.6km/1.6miles and then turn left over a bridge. Turn left immediately after it and fork right after 2.9km/1.8miles. Park after another 1.1km/0.7miles in a small carpark on the right (984 884) where forest continues on the left but ceases on the right.

On the side of the road opposite the carpark take the firebreak steeply downhill to the stream and up again to tarmac (use the stile). Cross the road and ascend, forest initially on the right, to Ballineddan (*Baile an fheadain*, Homestead of the Streamlet: 652m/2,151ft) which has a tiny cairn and gives a good foretaste of the views to be had further up.

The slight drop after Ballineddan preludes a steady climb with excellent underfoot conditions to Slievemaan. On the way you will pass a large heap of rocks which, having read this, you will not mistake in bad weather for Slievemaan itself. Slievemaan (*Sliabh meadhoin*, Middle Mountain: 759m/2,501ft) has a boggy undistinguished summit but the views, especially towards the nearby huge mound of Lugnaquilla, are superb.

The route continues to the southwest between two narrow but deeply incised streams. As you descend, note the thick stone walls enclosing fields ahead and try to pick a place which minimises wall-crossing and field-traversing (do both carefully!). The aim is to gain a crossways dirt track serving several farmhouses and to descend left from there to the 'main' road ('main' is purely relative) at the Army range warning sign.

Take the side road southwest opposite the main road, continue to the T and turn right to another 'main' road. Turn right here for the car but if you wish to take in Keadeen continue straight ahead (it's a crossroads off-set to the right) and walk to the end of the track, continue up the path beyond it to emerge into fields and then open ground.

The saddle between Carrig and Keadeen now lies directly ahead over rough heathery ground. At the saddle follow the wall, and the fence and earthbank further up north to the summit of Keadeen (*Ceidin*, Flat-topped Hill; 654m/2,146ft). Its isolated position ensures excellent views; in good visibility you should be easily able to see the cooling towers at Allenwood and even Portarlington, about 40km/25miles away. Particularly noteworthy is the great double-walled ring fort at Brusselstown Ring close below. How much more impressive it appears from here than from the Ring itself!

The descent is east along a set of wheel-marks which later improves to a track. Further down keep forest on the left all the way back to the start.

Distance: 16km/10miles. Ascent: 760m/2,500ft. Walking time: 6 hours.

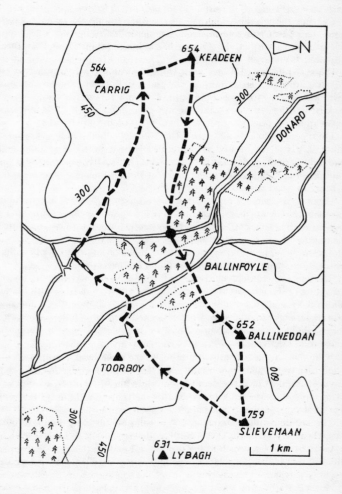

31. CIRCUIT OF THE OW VALLEY

This route, taking in Lugnaquilla and the Ow valley to its south is a long though not very demanding walk. The wide variety of scenery is unfortunately not matched by variety of slope — nearly all climb to Lug and nearly all descent after it. At least it has the virtue of simplicity.

Car only though this walk may also be done from Aghavannagh youth hostel. Drive to Drumgoff crossroads as described under Walk 23. From here drive for a further 9km/5miles to the hostel on the right. Park carefully near its entrance.

Walk about 1km/0.5miles west along the road to a road junction on the left. Turn right here through a gate and take the track beyond upwards towards a lonely farm overlooking the Ow valley. Fork left onto a minor track before the farm and continue upwards, forest on the left, towards the insignificant bump, simply labelled 1,008ft on the older maps.

From here on to Lybagh (631m/2,069ft) and beyond that to Slievemaan (759m/2,501ft) is a steady ascent with pleasant heathery ground and gradually widening views in all directions. Particularly noteworthy is the South Prison of Lug, whose initial formidable awesomeness increases even further as you advance.

Beyond Slievemaan the great bare rectangular bulk of Lugnaquilla dominates to the northeast, reached by a direct and obvious route, first a drop through peat hags (the one and only drop on this leg), then a sustained ascent through short, usually dry grass.

The summit of Lug is described under Walk 23; suffice to say here that the views are magnificent in good visibility and well worth studying.

The next target is Corrigasleggaun (794m/2,534ft) reached by a dexterous swing to the left round the precipitous periphery of the South Prison followed by a high level stroll, nearly all gently downhill. At the one junction take care to follow the Corrigasleggaun rather than the Clohernagh spur. A slight detour left to survey Kelly's Lough, which may be combined with a meal stop, makes a pleasant diversion.

South of Corrigasleggaun the aim is firstly to head towards Doyle Street (519m/1,702ft) on the spur directly east of the Ow River. Later, however, keep to its left side so as to pick up a forest track a little way down. This track curves downward round the spur though not with the degree of complexity shown on the 'Wicklow Way' map. Just before the first prominent bridge, take a branch heading down sharply to the right. This will take you through a pleasant stretch of mature forest and back to tarmac. Turn left for the car or the hostel.

Distance: 17.5km/11miles. Ascent: 720m/2,400ft. Walking time: 6½ hours.

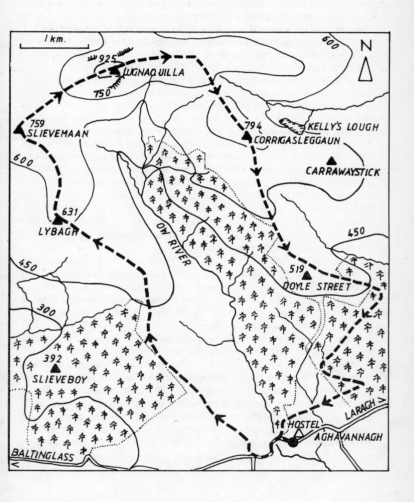

Reference OS Map: Wicklow Way (1:50,000).

32. CROGHAN MOUNTAIN

Lying astride the borders of counties Wicklow and Wexford, Croghan (locally Croaghan Kinsella) is a relatively distant outlier of the Wicklow Mountains. It is situated in a pleasant pastoral area with the valley of the Aughrim River to the north separating it from the bulk of the mountains. A varied scene therefore greets the walker on the way to or on the summit: pasture land and low hills near at hand, the southeast corner of the Wicklow Mountains — and indeed the Blackstairs further off to the southwest — rising beyond then.

By car drive to Aughrim on the R753 and then take the R747 (Tinahely road). Four km/2.5miles from Aughrim turn left (signposted 'Toberpatrick') and turn left again at the T. Turn sharply first right and park carefully at the second turn left (the first being a lane), less than 1km/0.5miles away at 104·744.

Walk along this left turn, a stony road which rapidly deteriorates to a muddy one. At the T negotiate as best you can the ploughed field ahead and cross the far ditch to reach open country with the northwest spur of Croghan rising near you on the left. Head for this spur and as you climb it look out for a wide winding track which will facilitate your ascent.

At the top of the spur an exceedingly short length of wall — or it could be a low cairn — is a useful landmark. Turn left (east) here and head for Croghan (*Cruachan*, Hill: 607m/1,993ft) along a very gradually rising stretch of moorland. The summit is unmistakable: a splendid assemblage of boulders and an inexplicably small trig. pillar.

From the top descend east to forest, keep it on the right and continue along its edge until the ground starts to drop. At this point head northeast to another block of forest and keep it on your left with upland fields on the right. Beyond this forest keep to the high ground to yet another block of forest whose nearest corner marks the undistinguished top of Ballinasilloge, the northeast spur of Croghan.

For the return retrace your steps to what is now the far end of the middle block of forest and prepare for some trackless navigation. At this far end descend east to a wall separating moorland from upland fields, turn left and proceed along a vestigial path past a trace of a corrie half-heartedly gouged into the northern side of Croghan. As you advance watch out for forest peeping over the low hill ahead and bounded on its left by a gigantic Great Wall of Croghan. Cross it where you can (carefully please), turn left and walk down to the T at the start of the walk. Turn right to face the muddy and subsequently stony track to the car.

Distance: 13km/8miles. Ascent: 520m/1,700ft. Walking time: 4½ hours.

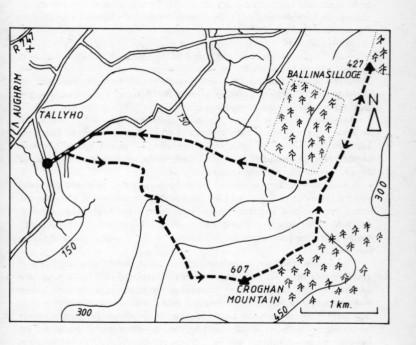

The map shows a route from TALLYHO (near AUGHRIM, R 747) passing south of BALLINASILLOGE (427) and up to CROGHAN MOUNTAIN (607). Contour lines mark 150, 300 and 450 metres.

1 km.

33. BLACKSTAIRS MOUNTAIN

*The 'tail' of the Blackstairs from its southern tip to the Scullogue Gap
is just one ridge wide. This ridge falls gradually to east and west into
the rich pastures of Wexford and Carlow. The walk described here covers the
northern end of the 'tail', that is the central section of the entire range, taking in
the granite tors around Caher Roe's Den and Blackstairs Mountain itself. It ends
with a pleasant stroll through country lanes.*

Drive to Ballymurphy, a village situated 4.5km/2.5miles west of the
Scullogue Gap on the R702 (the L30). From here take the road signposted
St Mullins and Glynn, turn left off it after 1.3km/0.8miles and continue
straight on for about another 1.6km/1mile to where the road swings sharply
right (792 451).

Walk the road to the nearby farmhouse continuing straight ahead
through the gate (leave it as you found it). The route from here ascends to
the low saddle to the southeast which can be seen in good weather from
about here and which can be reached without further recourse to tedious
directions and without crossing fences. Full (and tedious) bad weather
directions follow in the next paragraph.

Take the path beyond the gate to a lateral fence, by which stage you
will have noted that the path shows a marked disinclination to climb the
hillside. Turn left at this fence, cross a green track, ascend to another, turn
right to reach a formidable ruin and continue on from here on the track or
by any convenient route to the saddle.

At the saddle turn northeast onto the main ridge to climb the rock-
strewn shoulder of 553m/1,813ft, marked by a massive tor. Descend the
small drop beyond and then resume the upward and fairly steep climb to
Blackstairs Mountain, a climb enlivened by the spectacle of the rocky
teeth of granite protruding from its western flank (one of these is Caher
Roe's Den).

The summit of Blackstairs Mountain (734m/2,409ft) is a slight disap-
pointment: a small cairn set on a flat area of scattered peat hags. Beyond it
Mount Leinster, topped by its TV transmitter, dominates the view ahead
with Knockroe a nearer and lower rounded peak across Scullogue Gap.
The aim now is to walk over the northern shoulder of Blackstairs
Mountain towards Scullogue Gap and, once on the moderately steep drop
beyond it (the shoulder), to come north off the ridge. As you descend
watch out for a convenient place to reach the road below, either at a
laneway or by crossing one (preferably) rough field only.

On the road turn left and walk west along it for about 2km/1mile to
the crest of a low hill. The road swings sharply left here and as it resumes
its original direction, take a left turn onto a narrow road. This road, in
parts scarcely more than a lane, runs in a meandering course between
high hedges and stone walls and in its course passes through the tiny
hamlet of Walshstown nestling in a pronounced dip in otherwise

undulating terrain. Directions along here need be minimal only: continue straight ahead to the T and turn left here within a few hundred metres of the car.

Distance: 13km/8miles. Ascent: 640m/2,100ft. Walking time: 5 hours.

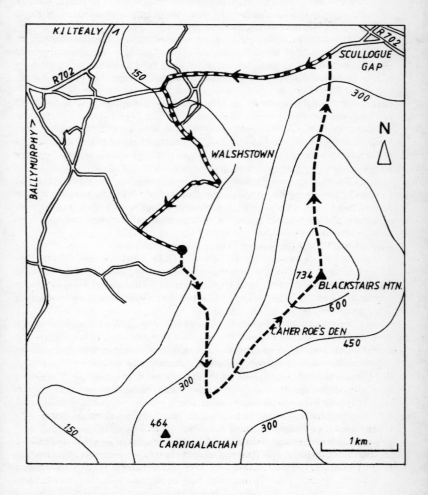

Reference OS Map: Sheet 19 (1:126,720).

34. MOUNT LEINSTER FROM THE SOUTH

From Scullogue Gap this walk takes in the broad ridge of bare heathery mountain to its north. The route is an unbroken climb to Mount Leinster except for the substantial drop north of rounded Knockroe. It culminates in Mount Leinster itself, at 796m/2,610ft the highest peak in the Blackstairs. The return is over its southwest spur, descending beyond it along the deeply incised valley of a minor tributary of the River Barrow.

Take the R702 (the L30) to the one and only crossroads (unsignposted) at the top of the rather indeterminate Scullogue Gap. Turn north here (i.e. right from the Kiltealy direction), and turn left at the T a short distance on, thus taking a side road to the north of and roughly parallel to the R702. From this T drive about 1.5km/1mile to the crest of the hill (806 492) and park near a convenient laneway or rough fields on the right to avoid crossing enclosed fields.

Walk diagonally right steeply uphill towards Knockroe (542m/1,777ft) through rough pathless rocky terrain aiming, as you advance, for the cross which, you may be heartened to learn, is very close to the top. Knockroe has a well-built cairn (plenty of raw material lying about), the outline of a house and even a rain gauge for good measure (both senses).

Heading north of Knockroe descend to the broad saddle between it and Mount Leinster, upland fields on the right, and cross a track coming up from Scullogue Gap. Continue up through high heather to the southern spur of Mount Leinster, descend sightly beyond the spur and then climb through boulders to the summit plateau.

Mount Leinster stands at the centre of four distinct spurs and as is appropriate to its height, commands good views over most of the Blackstairs, the south of the Wicklow Mountains, including pre-eminently Lugnaquilla, and a wide variety of low hill and agricultural country. Its attraction is, of course, severely diminished by the sore thumb of the TV transmitter though the associated buildings blend in quite well with their surroundings.

Boulders and steep ground slow progress initially on the descent southwest towards Crannagh mountain, which is but a slight rise, the huge array of boulders hereabouts being a clearer distinguishing mark. Veer left off the spur beyond Crannagh to walk parallel to the river. A wisp of a path between fields on one side and gorse close to the river on the other will help in finding an acceptable way through enclosed fields. Finally, and here a signpost in the near distance will be an indication that you are close to the road, follow the path down to the river, walk downstream on either bank, and gain the road. Turn left here and left again at the fork to reach the car.

Distance: 9km/6miles. Ascent: 750m/2,500ft Walking time: 4 hours.

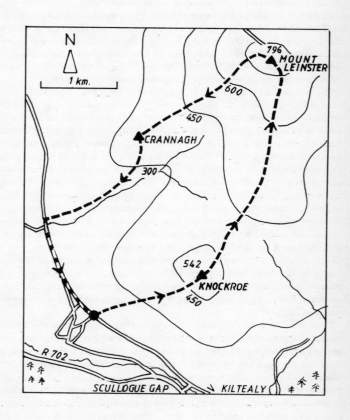

N

1 km.

796
MOUNT
LEINSTER

600

450

CRANNAGH

300

542

KNOCKROE

450

R 702

SCULLOGUE GAP

KILTEALY

Reference OS Map: Sheet 19 (1:126,720).

35. MOUNT LEINSTER AND BALLYCRYSTAL

The major exception to the general north-south trend of the Blackstairs is provided by the undulating spur reaching out east to Black Rock Mountain. This is probably the most interesting approach to Mount Leinster: the spur makes for a varied and scenic walk and after the slog south beyond it, the remote basin of Ballycrystal forms a leisurely end to an easy day.

When you have found the start of this walk, relax — most of your navigational problems are behind! From the village of Kiltealy take the R702 (the L30) towards Enniscorthy, branching left onto the R746 (the L32) towards Bunclody after just over 1.5km/1mile. Turn left at the multiple junction 2.6km/1.6miles further on and left again a few hundred yards on. Drive straight on for 2.6km/1.6miles and park at a forest entrance on the right just before a bungalow (at about 854 509).

Walk past the bungalow and the narrow strip of mature forest beyond it and turn right through a gate between the forest and a field. Walk to the top of the forest, pass through another gate and continue directly upwards to the crest of the ridge, picking up a useful track (but useful for a short time only) near the crest. The large flat-roofed stone building at the crest is worth inspecting. The summit of Black Rock lies a few hundred yards further east and is a there-and-back which may be visited by purists or those who do not intend to tell even little fibs about the mountains they climbed.

The rest of us will head directly west to Mount Leinster, climbing on the way a couple of rocky protuberances too modest to bother the contour lines of the maps. An area of strewn boulders beyond them marks the upper slopes of Mount Leinster.

From the summit, described under walk 34, head south along the spur ending in Knockroe keeping to the east side (of the spur). Here you may recoup the cost of this book by betting (but not too insistently, mind) that the track to which you are heading is not rising, though to the naked eye it certainly appears as if it is.

Take this track (and it is level!) to the south and then southeast and when it disappears collect your winnings and head down to the ruin with the two beautiful beech trees at the southwest corner of Ballycrystal (at this point the track has re-emerged and can be seen sneaking round to the ruin).

Take this track north (it shortly graduates to a narrow road) which a little way down passes through a region of pleasant forest. From here it is but a short walk through mixed farmland and forest back to the car.

Distance 9.5km/6miles. Ascent: 580m/1,900ft. Walking time: 4 hours.

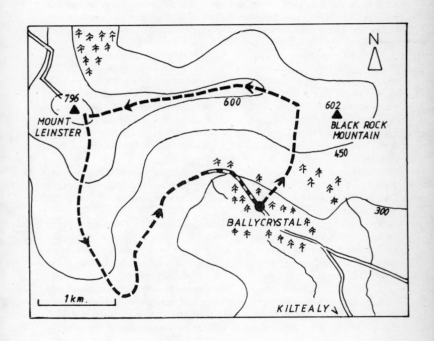

Reference OS Map: Sheet 19 (1:126,720).

SOUTH
Miriam Joyce McCarthy

INTRODUCTION

This guide is basically a series of route descriptions intended to help people find their way on and off the hills. It should be helpful to those new to hill walking or experienced walkers to this area. Of course, there are many routes and endless variations of those described.

The routes described range from short rambles along tracks to longer trips for experienced walkers with navigational skills.

The following walks are totally on tracks and enable one to experience a mountain environment without the associated risks:

Walks 36, 37, 43, 45 (B), 63 (B) and 67, have tracks leading all the way to the summits.

Walk 41 has a path and Walk 59 has a track leading to two spectacular corrie lakes. Walks 52 and 53 combine to make up the East Munster Way, a low-level way-marked trail.

Walks 54, 55 and 56: the first sections of these walks have tracks going well into the mountains to elevations of over 600m. All other routes are on open moorlands and should only be attempted to walkers with mountaineering skills.

It is advisable to walk the routes in the direction in which they are described to avoid any difficulties of access.

The southeast is covered by OS maps ½inch, Nos 22 and 18. Some minor roads and lanes are not shown. Neither are many of the newly planted and some not so new forests. Of course all forest roads are unmarked!

Hill walkers in the southeast have always enjoyed a special relationship with the local farming communities and this should be maintained by following the Country Code given at the beginning of this book.

In wishing you enjoyable and memorable walking, may I protect myself by saying that while in the preparation of this guide I have been as careful as possible, I take no responsibility for the reader's failure to travel in safety.

I wish to thank the many people who helped me in the completion of the guide. The members of the Peaks Mountaineering Club who walked with me and stood patiently while I took notes — James Bond, Ann Butler, Irish Butler, Breda Costigan, Mary Lonergan, Ellen O'Donnell, Jim O'Neill. I am grateful to Pat Holland for advice on the antiquities of the area. Many thanks to Tom Joyce who contributed the walks in the Slieve Blooms; to Niall Carroll and Tony O'Brien for their local knowledge and advice on the Comeraghs; to Sr Brendan Keating and Cait Ni Mhaolachtnaigh for material on local history. Thanks to Greg Kenny for his tape recorder and to Joss Lynam for his help during the preparation of the book.

I'm particularly grateful to Justin McCarthy my partner, for the benefit of his mountaineering experience and his extensive knowledge of the Galtees; for walking with me every Sunday and for his help, encouragement and understanding when the pressure was on.

Access and Accommodation

The mountains of the southeast of Ireland are very accessible both to the Irish hill walker and the visitor from abroad. There are passenger/car ferry services from Britain to Dun Laoghaire (Dublin) and Rosslare daily. Continental visitors can take the ferry direct to Rosslare from Le Havre or Cherbourg and be in the mountains within a few hours of arrival in the country. There are airports at Dublin, Cork and Waterford.

The area is well served by major roads. The N8 from Dublin to Cork runs through the region, and the Cahir to Mitchelstown section is parallel with the southern slopes of the Galty Ridge. The N8 also passes within a few kilometres of the Slieve Blooms at Portlaoise. The N24 from Limerick to Waterford passes close to the Galtees, Comeraghs and Slievenamon. The Silvermines and the Keeper Hill area can be approached from the N7 Dublin to Limerick route. The Knockmealdowns are within 20km of the N8 and N24 at Cahir, and are divided by one of the finest mountain passes in the country — the Vee on the R668 between Clogheen and Lismore.

The main railway line from Dublin to Cork also runs through the region, the most imposing sight during the journey being the superb backdrop of the Galty Mountains as the train pulls in to the busy station of Limerick Junction. Express buses run between the major towns but there is no public transport into the mountains.

Information on travel and accommodation can be obtained from the South-Eastern Tourism Organisation, whose head office is at 41 The Quay, Waterford, phone 051-75823. This office operates throughout the year but most towns have tourist information offices open to visitors during the summer months.

The southeast region is well endowed with accommodation of all types from Grade A hotels to country homes, hostels and caravans and camping parks.

The following is a small selection of places where mountaineers are especially welcome.

Town and Country Homes

  (i)   Hanoras Cottage, Nire Valley, Co. Waterford. 052-36134.
 (ii)   Mrs Ryan, Clonanav Farm House, Nire Valley,
        Co. Waterford. 052-36141.
(iii)   Homeleigh Farm House, Ballynacourty,
        Co. Tipperary. 062-56228.
 (iv)   Ballyglass House, Glen of Aherlow,
        Co. Tipperary. 062-52104.

Hostels

An Oige
  (i)   Ballydavid Wood, Youth Hostel, Glen of Aherlow, Bansha.
        Open 1 March–30 November. 062-54148.

(ii) Mountain Lodge, Youth Hostel, Burncourt, Cahir.
         Open 1 April–30 September. 052-67277.
  (iii) Lismore Hostel, Lismore.
         Open 1 April–30 September. 058-54390.

Private Hostels
   (i) Farmhouse Hostel, Cahir. 052-41906.
  (ii) Lisakyle, Cahir, Co. Tipperary.
        Open all year. 052-41963.
 (iii) Powers The Pot, Harney's Cross, South of Clonmel. 052-23085. The
        owner is an experienced mountaineer and his advice should be both
        appreciated and heeded. Open 1 March–23 December.

Caravan and Camping Parks
   (i) The Apple, on the N24 between Cahir and Clonmel. 052-41459.
  (ii) Ballynacourty House, Glen of Aherlow. 062-56230.
 (iii) Powers The Pot, Harney's Cross, South of Clonmel. 052-23085.

There are mountaineering clubs in Clonmel, Kilkenny and Waterford.
Their members walk these mountains regularly and the addresses and
telephone numbers of the current secretaries can be obtained from the
Mountaineering Council of Ireland, c/o AFAS, House of Sport, Longmile
Road, Dublin 12. 01-509845.

Geology
Were it not for the mountains and valleys we would not be able to enjoy
this exhilarating recreation. A little knowledge of what shaped the landscape will help one to appreciate their natural beauty and grandeur. The
study of the processes which shaped the landscape is that of a highly
complex and vast subject. In dealing with it I will attempt to be as simple
and straightforward as possible.

The highlands of the southeast of Ireland were formed about 300 million
years ago in the Devonian period when adjustments in the earth's crust
caused tremendous lateral pressuring to occur. These pressures forced the
crust to crumble into folds. Subsequent erosion of the higher folds has in
general caused the mountains as we know them. The extent of the erosion,
however, is dependent on the hardness of the rock at the top of the fold so
that in some cases the upward folds correspond with ridges of high relief
and in others they have been worn down completely to form valleys and
lowlands.

The high mountains of Waterford composed of old red sandstone (ORS)
overlook the coastal plains and the beautiful valley of the Blackwater
River. In the west the complex upfold corresponds with the Knockmealdown mountains; the Comeragh and Monavullagh mountains which lie
to the east of the Knockmealdowns are also composed of ORS, where

hundreds of metres of purple grits and brownish conglomerates and shales have been upfolded into a gigantic arch. The eastern end of the arch has been worn down to reveal a rolling plateau of silurian rocks, known as the plateau of Rathgormack — a fertile tract of farmland in contrast to the heathery hills of sandstone.

The Galtees, lying 32km/20miles north-northwest of the Comeraghs form a high ridge, in contrast to the plateau of the latter group. Rising abruptly from the plain of Tipperary with high grassy peaks and deep gullies, the Galtees form a very imposing group. Devonian folding has caused the ORS to protrude through its covering of carboniferous limestone and silurian rocks to protrude in their turn through the ORS so the high ground is formed of conglomerates and shales. One of the most striking characteristics of the Tipperary landscape is the way in which the landforms alternate between the slate and sandstone of the hills while the valleys and plains are composed largely of limestone. The famous Mitchelstown Caves owe their origin to the soluble properties of carboniferous limestone.

The streams which drain the corries of the Galtees flow steeply down the northern slopes into the picturesque Glen of Aherlow, once famed for its forest cover but now occupied by prosperous farmland on the limestone soil. The woodlands are now of the coniferous variety and are state plantations. The wooded Slievenamuck ridge forms the northern side of the glen.

Like the plateau of Rathgormack the anticlinal arch of Slievenamon has been breached on its eastern side to uncover silurian grits and slates, overlooked in the west by the steep sided dome of Slievenamon itself where the old red sandstone rises to 722m/2,368ft. The Devil's Bit mountain, the Silvermines and Keeper Hill in north Tipperary were also formed by folding in the Devonian period and are composed of sedimentary rocks similar to the mountains further south.

The ridge of the Slieve Blooms in Laois/Offaly contains the most northerly anticlines of the Armorican foldings in the southern half of Ireland. The carboniferous limestone has since been worn down to expose the underlying sandstone and slates. The highest point of this range is Arderin (528m/1,733ft) which, like all mountains of the Devonian period, has been lowered drastically by weathering and erosion in the 300 million years since being formed.

The direction of the folding in Munster is generally east-west and is termed the Armorican trend because it can be traced in the rocks of Armorica (Brittany). The north-east, south-west trend of the Caledonian period of mountain buildings (associated with the northern half of the country) can be seen in the north-south axis of the Comeraghs.

But it was the action of glaciers during the Ice Age which carved the most spectacular features of the Irish mountains and which gives them their greatest appeal. (It began 1 million years ago and lasted until 10,000 years ago.)

The Galtees, Knockmealdowns and Comeraghs were too high to be over-ridden by the inland ice-sheets but they had their own local glaciers. The higher peaks protruded above the ice-sheets as nunataks and were subjected to the constant severe frost shattering causing the rocks to fissure into grotesquely shaped outcrops. Particularly good examples are O'Loughnan's Castle, west of Greenane on the Galty Ridge and the summit of the Galtymore itself.

The eastern and northern faces of the Comeraghs have been extensively gouged out by a series of local glaciers leaving behind several superb corries, precipitous cliffs, glaciated valleys, hanging valleys and waterfalls. The gigantic amphitheatre of Coumshingaun is one of the finest examples of a corrie in these islands and has a back wall which rises 500m/1,700ft vertically above the lake, exposing a considerable part of the old red sandstone layers. The valley southwest of the gap is a hanging valley though not as spectacular as the Eagles Nest in the Magillycuddy Reeks; while the glaciated valley of Coumiarthar contains a series of small rock-basin lakes in hollows deepened by glacier which once occupied it.

The material excavated by the ice was deposited on the valley slopes as moraine and now often acts as a dam trapping a lake behind it. Good examples are to be found in the Galtees and Comeraghs.

After the glacial period, Ireland experienced a mild wet climate and forest and peat bogs became extensive. Only a small amount of natural oak forest remains — near Cahir — but the mountains contain vast areas of heather-clad blanket bogs.

Flora and Fauna

Flora With the exception of a few notable areas where a combination of particular conditions have provided a rich habitat — Mount Brandon in Co. Kerry is a good example — there is on Irish mountains a relative scarcity of species which in Britain, for instance, are more common. This certainly applies in the southeast where hills are covered by a blanket of species of poor acid grassland having as its main components common bent grass (*Agrostis tenuis*), wavy hair grass (*Deschampsia flexuosa*), sheep's fescue (*Festuca ovina*), sorrel (*Rumex acetosa*), sheep's sorrel (*R. acetosella*), heath bedstraw (*Galium saxatile*), bell heather (*Erica cinerea*), deer grass (*Scripus cespitosus*) and ribbed sedge (*Carex binervis*). Sundew (*Drosera*), an insectivorous plant, can be found in wet flushes.

However it has been claimed that botanical surveys of Irish mountain regions derive a peculiar zest from the very poverty of flora in alpine species (Nathaniel Colgan in *The Irish Naturalist*, 1900) and if this is accepted the corries of both the Galtees and the Comeraghs have much to excite the botanist. The former in particular provide interesting outlying stations for St Patrick's cabbage (*Saxifraga spathularis*) — one of the Lusitanian species of the Irish flora and a relative of the urban London Pride — the mossy saxifrages (*S. rosacea* and *S. hypnoides*) and mountain sorrel (*Oryria digyna*).

St Patrick's cabbage, which has an otherwise limited distribution in southwest Europe, has its main stations in south and west Ireland and in the Galtees is reported from Loughs Muskry and Borheen.

The mossy saxifrages occur at all the Galty corries as do green spleenwort (*Asplenium viride*) and cowberry (*Vaccinium vites idaea*), whilst mountain sorrel and dwarf willow (*Salix herbacea*) are missing only from Lough Borheen which is the least alpine in character. Other species of interest growing mainly by Loughs Curra and Muskry, but also beneath the bluffs on the northern side of the Carrignabinna/Lyracappul ridge, are brittle bladder fern (*Cystopteris fragilis*), rose root (*Rhodiola rosea*), filmy fern (*Hymenophyllum wilsonii*) and scurvy grass (*Cochlearia officinalis*). Strangely alpine saw-wort (*Saussurea alpina*) is reported as occurring only at the rather gloomy Lough Diheen though here limited botanical exploration of the range could be the reason.

In the Comeraghs the same factors of silurian shale cliffs facing generally away from the sun and the lack of grazing combine to make the corries the most interesting ground for the botanist. Coumshingaun is the main centre, for St Patrick's cabbage, mossy saxifrage (*hypnoides* but not *rosacea*), rose root, Welsh poppy (*Meconopsis cambrica*) and marsh hawks-beard (*Crepis paludosa*) all occur there, and St Patrick's cabbage also grows close to Crotty's Lake and Coumduala.

Due to the relative absence of suitable cliffs the Knockmealdowns are much poorer botanically than the Galtees and Comeraghs, though the broken ground north of the main summit again yields St Patrick's cabbage and mossy saxifrage (*S. hypnoides*). Further west the great banks of rhodo-dendrons (*R. ponticum*) rising almost vertically behind Bay Lough are a familiar sight to thousands of travellers, for the Vee Gap road runs along the opposite side of the valley.

The hills of north Tipperary are also of little interest to the botanist, the only notable plant of the area being cowberry on Keeper Hill. Hay-scented buckler fern (*Dryopteris aemula*) and mountain fern (*Thelypteris limbosperma*) also occur both here and on the Silvermines ridge, and the lesser twayblade orchid (*Listera cordata*) is the other species growing on both sides of the Mulkeir valley.

One of the most attractive spots in the Slieve Bloom is just north of Arderin, where valleys from each side of the range meet to form the Glendine Gap. It is also the most botanically rewarding spot in the range for Welsh poppy and the two ferns mentioned above are found close by. The peat bog which covers these hills is otherwise uninteresting, and the same can be said of Slievenamon which has only stiff sedge (*Carex bigelowii*) growing on the stony ground close to the summit.

Personally I have a great liking for the late summer flowering rowan tree (or mountain ash, *Sorbus aucuparia*) which grows by most of the valley streams in the region, though less frequently in the Comeraghs. I must admit also to less affection for whortleberries (*Vaccinium myrtillus*) which are plentiful almost everywhere, and which until a few years ago were picked and exported to South Wales as an energy food for miners. Driving around the lanes close to the Monavullaghs will be made all the more pleasant by the presence of fuchsia (*F. magellanica*) which though not as verdant here as in the west is just as welcome.

The lower slope of all the ranges are heavily forested. There is unquestionably a certain monotony in passing through these almost totally coniferous plantations but from the hilltops they add variety to the otherwise regular pattern of fields. Sitka spruce, imported from north America because of its remarkable growth record in poor soil, is the most common tree in these forests, often accompanied by Douglas fir, Scots pine, Norwegian spruce and larch. Sadly there are relatively few deciduous trees, though traces of the great forests which once completely covered the area can still be seen in the Glen of Aherlow. Scaragh Wood near Cahir has patches of natural oak and its associated ground flora.

Fauna   The fauna of Ireland is much less well documented than the flora, particularly when one attempts to relate it to a particular geographic feature such as mountains. There are, however, certain species of birds and animals which are known to be present generally and these, augmented by some personal sightings, form the basis for the notes which follow.

On the moorlands, and particularly on the less desolate hillsides, one invariably meets the ubiquitous skylark (*Alauda arvensis*), whilst yellowhammers (*Emberiza citrinells*), meadow pipits (*Anthus pratensis*), pied wagtails (*Motacilla alba*), stonechats (*Saxicola torquata*) and the occasional grey wagtail (*M. cinerea*) also tend to favour this type of terrain. Another attractive bird often seen in bracken or rushes is the hen harrier (*Circus cyaneus*) which breeds around the edge of forestry plantations and has a predilection for red sandstone areas. Game such as grouse (*Lagopus lagopus*) and pheasants (*Phasianus colchicus*) prefer blanket bog and sparse heather — the former are particularly numerous in the Slieve Blooms — and damp moorland is also favoured by curlews (*Numenius arquata*) which are now much less common than a few years ago. Short turf such as that grazed by sheep attracts wheatears (*Oenanthe oenanthe*), whilst scree slopes and crags are the habitat of ravens (*Corvus corax*), jackdaws (*Corvus monedula*) and the rare kestrels (*Falco tinnunculus*) and peregrine falcons (*Falco peregrinus*). Other birds of prey which frequent the region are merlins (*Falco columbarius*) and, generally at lower levels, sparrowhawks (*Accipiter nisus*). When walking by the mountain streams you may also have the pleasure of seeing the fascinating dippers (*Cinclus cinclus*, there is an Irish subspecies) which are present throughout the region though I have observed them only in the Comeraghs. This may be due to their early nesting, in February or March, and the early breeding of the ring ouzel (*Turdus torquatus*) may also account for the lack of recent information on this now relatively rare visitor.

I should also record that there is a chance of seeing herons (*Ardea cinerea*) in the mountains too. Mention should be made of the hooded or grey carrion crows (*Corvus corone cornix*) which are present in large numbers on all the lower slopes.

The only reptile in Ireland is the common or viviparous lizard (*Lacenta vivapara*) whilst insectivores are represented by hedgehogs (*Erinaceous europaeus*) and pygmy shrews (*Sorex minutus*) though there is little information as to the height at which these may be encountered. There is a very interesting concentration of wood ants (*Formica lugubris*) in the forests on both sides of the Galtees, for though there are a few nests in the woods of the northern Knockmealdowns, they are extremely rare elsewhere in Ireland. It is now considered possible that they were introduced into the dense woods of Tipperary as a food for pheasants.

The mammals include the nocturnal — and thus rarely seen — badger (*Meles meles*) and the far-ranging red fox (*Vulpes vulpes*) which can be spotted regularly up to the highest reaches of all the southeastern mountains. Fallow deer (*Dama dama*) occur in the woods on the slopes of the Galtees, Knockmealdowns and Comeraghs. The best time of the day to see them is at dawn or dusk. There is, however, a large herd of feral goats (*Capra*) on Slievenamuck and there are also goats — large in size if not in number — on the Knockmealdowns. Mountain hares (*Lepus timidus hibernicus*) are commonly seen at height on all the hills whilst in the limestone valley rabbits (*Oryctolagus cuniculus*) show many signs of recovery from the myxomatosis virus of the 1950s. And as you make your way through the forests you may be fortunate enough to see the delightful red squirrel (*Sciurus vulgaris leucourus*) or less likely the unobtrusive pine marten (*Martes martes*). Other mammals which should be mentioned are woodmice (*Apodemus sylvaticus*), which are found on many mountains, and brown rats (*Rattus norvegicus*) which are now unfortunately so numerous as to require very thorough control.

Fishing stories relating to mountains seem to be no less embellished that those elsewhere and I have often heard of gigantic trout (*Salmo trutta fario*) being taken from the Galty and Comeragh lakes. The fish are certainly there but, in my experience, gigantic they most definitely are not! There is also an interesting old record of char (*Salvelinus alpinus*), a fish belonging to colder climates but left in isolated localities since the glacial period, emanating from the Coumalocha on the western edge of the Comeraghs.

Given reasonable conditions butterflies can often be found on the highest summits, so although recording applies in the main to lower levels there is a reasonable guide to the possibility of finding certain species when hill walking. The speckled wood (*Pararge aegeria*), wall brown (*Pararge megera*), meadow brown (*Maniola jurtina*), small heath (*Coenonymphia pamphilus*), ringlet (*Aphantopus hyperanius*), small tortoiseshell (*Anglais urticae*), and large, small and green-veined white (*Pieris brassicae, rapae* and *napi*) are common almost everywhere, whilst the hedgebrown (*Maniola tithonus*) and dark green fritillary (*Argynnis aglaja*) are more likely to be seen around the Monavullaghs. The specialist may also be able to spot the grayling (*Eumenis semile*), common blue (*Polyommatus icarus*), small copper (*Lycaena phlaeas*), green hairstreak (*Callophrys rubi*) or marsh fritillary (*Euphydryas aurina*) though the latter is rather rare even on the boggy areas which are its habitat.

It will be apparent from the foregoing that information regarding discoveries and sightings of both fauna and flora is still extremely generalised. Botanists, lepidopterists or other naturalists visiting the area would thus perform a most useful service by specifically cataloguing their findings and forwarding them to the relevant authority, the Irish Biological Records Centre, St Martin's House, Waterloo Road, Dublin 4. And finally please remember that all of nature's works are seen to best advantage in their own setting and should therefore not be disturbed or interfered with in any manner whatsoever.

Antiquities

The story of man's involvement with the southeast of Ireland and its mountains seem to have begun about 4000 BC when the first farmers came to the country. Few traces of their settlement have survived though a good number of their tools, such as polished stone axeheads, are known.

The stone tombs in which they buried their dead remain, however. There is a passage tomb at Slievenamuck overlooking the Glen of Aherlow from the north and perhaps also under hilltop cairns such as those at Temple Hill, Slievenamon and Knockshanahullion.

Monuments of the succeeding Bronze Age (*c.* 2500 BC–300 BC) in which man began the use of metal, include stone tombs and there are several wedge tombs and a stone circle in the Silvermines. Standing stones like that associated with a burial site at the Barnamadra gap or close to the Nire Valley carpark may date from the Bronze Age.

Settlements of the Iron Age, the period traditionally associated with the Celts, may include some of the many ring-forts visible from the mountains.

Later in the fifth century AD we begin to enter the region of written history with the introduction of Christianity. The mountain routeway known as Rian Bo Phadraig which leads over the Knockmealdowns is supposed to have linked Cashel with Lismore. Routeways such as this may be of greater age and could even date back to prehistoric times. They were used up until comparatively recent times, before the advent of motorised transport.

Traces of the recent past, such as potato ridges indicating the terrible pressure for arable land in the last century, can be seen on the slopes of the Galtees.

Key Map

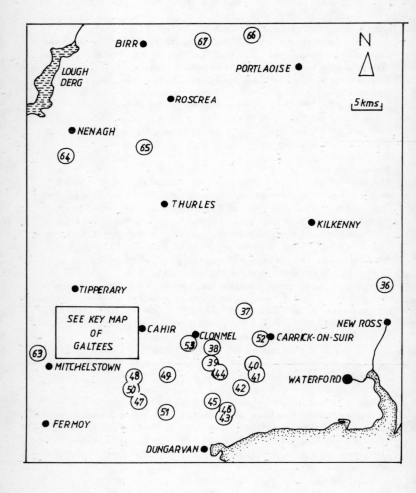

36. BRANDON HILL

On the west side of the River Barrow the clear-cut cone of Brandon Hill rises from the river bank to 516m/1,703ft. It forms part of the southern edge of the granitic mass of the Leinster Chain. The wooded slopes of Brandon give an added charm to the little town of Graiguenamanagh nestling by the river at its foot. Its summit is a fine viewpoint and it is an ideal hill on which to take the family along for a stroll.

Take the Inistioge road out of Graiguenamanagh and after 3.8km/2.4miles you will come to a lane on your left (not marked on ½ inch map) with a derelict house at the entrance (a short distance before the bridge). Drive up this lane, which is rough in spots, to a forestry barricade, 1.3km/0.8miles, where there is parking for three or four cars.

Walk up along a forestry road to where it forks. Take the left option and continue along this road around the head of the valley, then through a short pathway and finally out on the open moorland. There are lovely views of Graiguenamanagh beneath you through the mature forest.

When you emerge from the forest, bear right along the forest edge and right again along a track for a few minutes. Then go uphill along the spur for about 120m/400ft towards the large steel cross (erected by the people of Graiguenamanagh). The summit cairn is just behind the cross.

The views from here are superb, the River Barrow meandering peacefully beneath you, the Wicklow and Blackstairs ranges to the northeast and east. On a clear day you can see as far as Waterford Harbour and Hook Head.

Descend by retracing your steps or by following the track which descends from the summit along the western edge of the forest to where you join the forest road again.

Distance: 6.4km/4miles. Ascent: 330m/1,100ft. Walking time: 2/2½ hours.

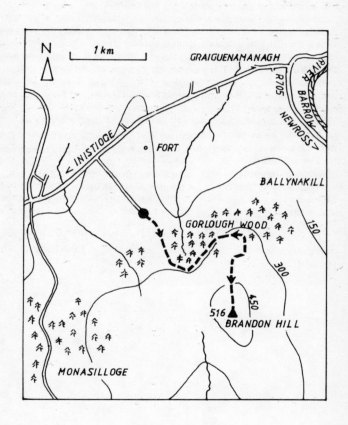

Reference OS Map: Sheet 19 (1:126,720).

37. SLIEVENAMON

(Sliabh na mBan, Mountain of the Women of Fionn)

According to the legend the large cairn on the summit of this great sandstone cone is where Fionn Mac Cumhaill sat waiting for Grainne, daughter of the High King, Cormac Mac Airt. They were in love and wished to marry but Fionn was so popular with the ladies, the King decided that there would be a race up these slopes and whoever reached the top first would win his hand. Fionn showed Grainne a short cut up the mountain and she was victorious.

The ascent from Kilcash 314 280 is very straightforward and requires no navigational skills as the route is entirely on a track.

To get to the starting point take the N24 and N76 from Clonmel. After about 13km/8miles turn left towards the village of Ballypatrick, at which you turn right for Kilcash. Drive through Kilcash and turn left at the top of the hill. About 400m/0.25miles past a sharp right-hand bend there is a farmyard. Park here, 317 289.

Take the lane on the left-hand side of the road. Follow this lane through a gate and out on to the open mountain. Here, bear right and follow a new track with a wood on your right. Continue on this track up to the summit cairn 719m/2,368ft.

Near the summit you will come across an unsightly building which bears testimony to local needs for multi-channel television.

Retracing your steps offers an excellent opportunity to enjoy the unique vista of the Suir Valley.

Distance: 5km/3miles. Ascent: 480m/1,600ft. Walking time:2½ hours

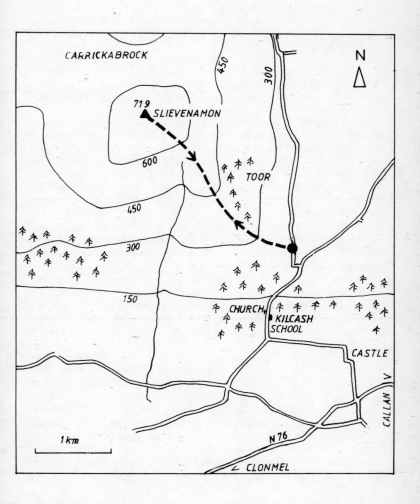

CARRICKABROCK

450

300

N

719
SLIEVENAMON

600

450

TOOR

300

150

CHURCH
KILCASH
SCHOOL

CASTLE

CALLAN V

1 km

N 76

CLONMEL

Reference OS Map: Sheet 18 (1:126,720).

105

38. LONG HILL AND LAGHTNAFRANKEE

The northern foothills of the Comeraghs fall directly towards the valley of the Suir and the town of Clonmel. It is a very accessible and popular walking area among the local inhabitants.

There are traces of old routes marked on the map and discernible on the ground — linking Clonmel with the villages of Glenary, Glendalough and the Nire Valley.

The walk I have chosen to describe takes in Long Hill, the Glenary River and Laghtnafrankee.

Take the R678 east from Clonmel and after about 5km/3miles just past the entrance to the golf club park by a gate leading in to the forest on your right, 238 196.

Walk directly along the forest road towards the head of the valley to emerge into the punchbowl, a large natural amphitheatre. Turn right along the outside of the forest. Then, shortly, bear left and walk up to the top of the ridge using a small cairn as your target. As you walk westwards towards Long Hill 385m/1,273ft you will see the lush farmland of the Suir Valley and the town of Clonmel with its expanding suburbs just beneath you to the north. Along here also you will see low pillars marking a former firing range.

Descend 100m/300ft to a col. A few hundred metres to the northwest is a large cross and altar erected in 1956 by the people of the Old Bridge area of Clonmel. You may wish to detour to it. (One can descend directly to Clonmel from the cross.)

Return to the col and then southwest to the ruins of what must have been a beautifully situated farm. This is an ideal spot to take a break.

Proceed southwards towards the Glenary River by staying right of a forestry plantation going downhill. Cross the river by the stepping stones. Just west of here is the old deserted village of Glenary — today a lonely forgotten place which may be tedious to reach from this side.

Keep the forest on your right as you begin to go uphill again. When you get above the trees you will arrive at the first of two cairns from which you must turn east along the top of another broad ridge. Running at right angles to your route is the dramatic northern Comeragh Ridge culminating in Knockanaffrin, while below you to the south are the picturesque woods of the Nire Valley and the village of Glendalough. After passing the 428m/1,404ft point, bear left slightly downhill to a minor col crossing an old route known as the Staire. This old route, discernible in places on the ground, connected the Nire with Clonmel. Then 120m/130yds of uphill will take you to the triangulation point and cairns at the summit of Laghtnafrankee, 518m/1,710ft.

The direct route back to your car is to head due north down into the punchbowl and the forest.

Distance: 10km/6miles. Ascent: 450m/1,500ft. Walking time: 3½ hours.

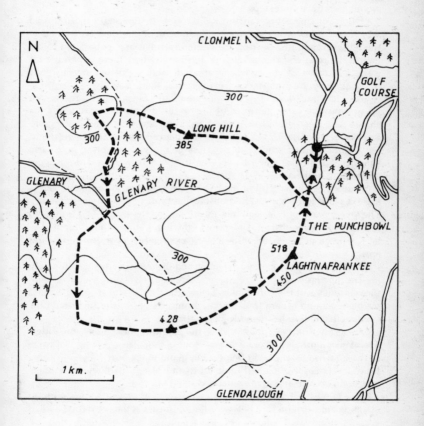

CLONMEL

GOLF
COURSE

300

LONG HILL
385

GLENARY

GLENARY RIVER

300

THE PUNCHBOWL

518
LAGHTNAFRANKEE
450

428

300

1 km.

GLENDALOUGH

Reference OS Map: Sheet 22 (1:126,720).

107

39. KNOCKANAFFRIN RIDGE

This ridge is known locally as the 'Seven Sisters' because of its rocky outcrops when viewed from the eastern side. Though there are limited opportunities for easy scrambling it is a fine invigorating but easy walk.

The starting point I prefer is at Glenanore 263 145 which enables you to enjoy this lovely ridge walk and be able to return to your car without having to retrace your steps.

From Ballymacarbry (on the R671 south of Clonmel) take the road which goes eastwards along the southern bank of the River Nire (Nier) to the Nire Church. Just beyond the church turn left and go straight to the end of the road and the village of Glenanore, where there is parking for just a few cars. This village was far more densely populated in years gone by, judging by the number of deserted houses there now.

A rough track leads towards the mountains from the village. As you set off you will catch glimpses of the ridge through the trees. Cross the stream and head uphill in a northeast direction over grassy slopes to Knocksheegowna, 679m/2,181ft. As you pause for a breather you might see traditional turf cutting in progress below you in spring and early summer. Laghtnafrankee can be seen to the northwest and the Knockmealdowns and Galtees in the distance.

Knocksheegowna (Hill of the Fairy Calves) is soon encountered and is a good place to take a rest and absorb the beauty of your surroundings. The lovely name of this peak (not mentioned on the ½ inch OS) is derived from a legend about the lake below to the left, Lough Mohra, reputed to be the home of a herd of milk-white cows tended by a beautiful water sprite.

This ridge makes for easy navigation and the direction is generally south.

The northeast slopes are steep, boulder-strewn and wooded, with pleasant views of the corrie lakes below, the first of which soon becomes visible — Lough Mohra (*Loch Mor* — ironically one of the smallest in the Comeraghs) in the shadow of Knockanaffrin.

Knockanaffrin, 753m/2,478ft, is the highest point along the ridge. Translated, it means Hill of the Mass — one of two places bearing that name in the Comeraghs, the other being a townland in the Nire Valley. In penal times Irish people often had to resort to an isolated townland or a lonely mountain peak to attend mass in peace.

The peak itself is a jumble of fractured conglomerate rock with an insignificant cairn on top. Below to the southeast is the second lake-filled corrie, Coumduala (Hollow of the Black Cliff).

Descending from the top you will soon be skirting the dangerous cliffs over Coumduala along a well-worn path which leads down to the Gap. From here on a sunny winter's day the coums of the Comeraghs present a very impressive picture — from Crotty's Rock in the east to the Sgilloge lakes in the west.

The Gap itself had an old route running through it — which can still be discerned — from the Nire Valley to Rathgormack.

Return to Glenanore by the lower western slopes of the ridge. Pass along the spur which descends from Knockanaffrin and head towards the stream you crossed at the start of the walk. Pick up the track and return to Glenanore.

Distance: 11km/7miles. Ascent: 580m/1,900ft. Walking time: 4hours.

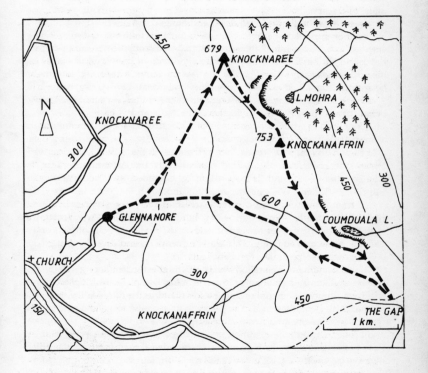

Reference OS Map: Sheet 22 (1:126,720).

40. CROTTY'S LAKE

William Crotty, a highwayman, was the leader of a gang of outlaws in the eighteenth century who used the Comeraghs as their base. Even the OS has agreed to accept the name for the lake and the outstanding pinnacle above it. He harassed the countryside from the Comeraghs to the coast. He robbed the rich and gave to the poor and accumulated a considerable treasure for himself. The mountainside was his refuge — in a cave beside the lake. It was known only to his wife and himself and could only be entered by way of a 'chimney' climb.

His look-out point was an outstanding pinnacle on the northeast edge of Comeraghs just above the lake itself — now called Crotty's Rock. From here he could easily spot soldiers toiling up the slopes, in plenty of time to make his escape.

Crotty was finally captured, tried and hanged in Waterford in 1742 on information supplied by David Norris — one of his faithful band of followers — who betrayed him. Afterwards Norris, afraid of revenge and perhaps hoping to lay his hands on some of Crotty's hidden treasures, persuaded the authorities to put a price on the outlaw's widow. After being pursued by soldiers, she killed herself by jumping to her death from Crotty's Rock.

Crotty's Lake, the scene of these tragic happenings, is one of the most beautiful and peaceful places in the Comeraghs and is easily accessible. The lake itself is a fine one with towering cliffs rising above it though not as high as those at Coumshingaun.

From Ballyhest crossroads 368 154 on the R676 (Carrick-on-Suir to Dungarvan road), take the second road on the right. After about 0.8km/ 0.5miles there is a rough layby on the right opposite double farm gates 348 136. Park here. Walk up the road for another 800m/0.5mile, take the rough track on your left, past a small stream to a new forestry road on the right. Walk uphill along this road, gaining height easily. At a junction under the hill, turn right towards a wall and fence. There are ruins of an old sheep pen on your right. This wall and fence ascend directly along the edge of the moraine to the corrie above.

Here you will have a splendid view of the spectacular Crotty's Rock. It can be reached by one of several routes. One way is to walk up along a heathery slope and emerge on top, beside the large boulders at the base of the rock.

The most interesting route, in my opinion, is to follow a sheep track and broken fence in the direction of a short gully with a pillar on its right. Pass below this pillar and ascend a broad, steep, easy gully which will take you to Crotty's Rock without too much difficulty. On emerging from the gully turn left to the large outcrop of conglomerate rock which is Crotty's. Take note of the low arch in the outcrop. The story goes that after going through this arch the first person you meet will be your life's partner!

You are now on the desolate Comeragh plateau. Proceed in a westerly direction to the top of a steep, glaciated valley which contains a group of small, beautiful and lonely lakes. They are marked but not named on the ½ inch OS map. The largest of these is called Coumgorra, the Lake of the Echoes. A tributary of the Clodiagh River flows out of these lakes. You can descend close to them by taking the eastern spur.

Eventually you will have to contour back to Crotty's Lake — the western edge, where you will be able to enjoy once more the solitude of this splendid coum. From here retrace your steps back to civilisation.

Distance: 8km/5miles. Ascent: 640m/2,100ft. Walking time: 3½ hours.

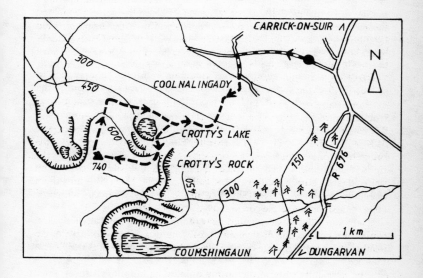

Reference OS Map: Sheet 22 (1:126,720).

111

41. THE CIRCUIT OF COUMSHINGAUN

The gigantic glacial amphitheatre of Coumshingaun (Hollow of the Ants) is claimed to be the finest example of a corrie in these islands. Situated very close to the main road, it is a perfect place to experience a mountain environment with very little effort.

The lake itself, the largest in the Comeraghs, is said to be 'bottomless and containing evil spirits'! Less than one hour's walk from the road, it is a popular location for family picnics. The towering cliffs rising above the lake have many rock-climbing routes, most of which get infrequent ascents.

The route around the encircling coum is perhaps the finest and most invigorating walk in the Comeragh mountains. The southern ridge offers some enjoyable but easy scrambling, the nearest thing to the Kerry Reeks in this part of the country.

The starting point 350 116 is close to a bridge on the R676 about 14km/9miles south of Carrick-on-Suir. The bridge is over the stream which flows down from the lake. Park close to the junction of a minor road.

Enter by a gate across the main road and follow the track down to the stream and across a grassy field and some scrub. (The area inside the gate tends to be very muddy in winter. In these circumstances, the alternative route is through a large field just south of the gate.)

Cross the stile out onto the open mountain and follow a clear path in the direction of the corrie. This path continues underneath the end of the north shoulder and on to the lake. From the lake take the southern spur and then along the arête. As you move along, doing some mild scrambling, you will be rewarded by spectacular and plunging views down both sides — glimpses of the lake beneath you to your right as you move around the rocks and views into a deep narrow valley on the opposite side.

These rocks lead to a grassy section with a sheep track to the left of the crest. The last scramble up to the plateau must be taken with great care and is not at all suitable for inexperienced walkers. Once on the plateau you will be able — on a clear day — to see the Waterford and Wexford coastlines.

You may wish to detour towards Fauscoum, 789m/2,597ft, the small cairn which represents the highest point in the Comeraghs. Fauscoum rises only a few metres above the surrounding boggy plateau and may be difficult to locate.

Back to the cliff edge again — head around the rim of the corrie toward the grassy cone of *Staicin-min*, 703m/2,308ft, Smooth Peak. Proceed along the northern spur keeping the stream *'Uisce Solais'* (Water of Light, not named on ½ inch map) on your left.

Descend carefully over rough terrain, taking care not to leave the spur too early and end up on steep ground over the lake.

When you finally reach the vicinity of the lake you deserve a rest and an opportunity to admire the splendour of Coumshingaun, and retrace with your eyes the route you have just taken. You must eventually drag yourself away from the serenity of this place and head back to the hustle and bustle of civilisation.

Distance: 8km/5miles. Ascent: 700m/2,300ft. Walking time: 4 hours.

B. To the lake and back.

Distance: 4km/2.5miles. Ascent: 250m/800ft. Walking time: 1¾ hours.

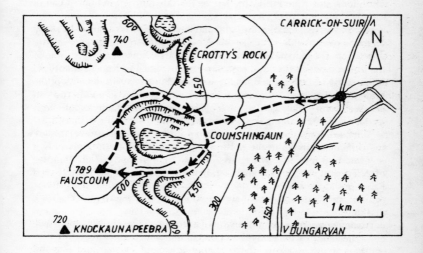

Reference OS Map: Sheet 22 (1:126,720).

42. THE MAHON FALLS AND COUMTAY

The upper section of the Mahon River is a rugged and beautiful place in the Comeragh Mountains. This broad glaciated valley has a large stream, the sources of which rise in the desolate plateau above, before converging and tumbling down in a series of spectacular cascades with precipitous walls. In summer it forms rock pools with just a trickle of water flowing over the boulders but in winter it falls in a really impressive drop of around 150m/500ft.

It can be reached by turning west off the R676 (north of Dungarvan) at Mahon Bridge (Furraleigh) 343 060. Turn right immediately by a shop following the signs for 'Comeragh Drive'. In a little over 1.5km/1mile turn right along a road (not marked on ½ inch OS) with the Mahon River on your right. Park in the car park just under the col 315 080.

Two large boulders mark the footpath which leads directly to the bottom of the falls. Cross the stream over the stepping stones where the footpath meets the stream. (N.B. It is sometimes impassable in wet winter conditions and climbing to the left of the falls is not advisable.) Climb steeply along faint tracks with the falls on your left.

Cross the river above the falls and head uphill in a south-westerly direction over a wide plateau with the infant Mahon tributaries draining down from the marshes and peat hags. The area, however, offers some of the finest views in the southeast. The majestic cone of Knockaunapeebra 720m/2,384ft is behind you, while southwards you have fine views of the Waterford coastline and Dungarvan Bay — if the day is good! You can also see Seefin 725m/2,387ft, the highest point of the Monavullaghs with its ugly building spoiling this wilderness area.

Further along the route you will approach the narrow neck where the cliffs of Coumfea to the north and Coumtay to the south are only a few hundred metres/yards apart. On your way you will catch glimpses of Slievenamon, Knockanaffrin and, in the distance, the Galtees and Knockmealdowns.

Turn in the direction of Coumtay. Circle around the edge of the cliffs and only begin to lose height when you reach the far end of the southern encircling spur. When you drop down to the end of the spur turn left and cross the valley by the ruins of an isolated house.

Walk uphill along the forest edge and back along the road to rejoin your car.

Distance: 11km/6½ miles. Ascent: 400m/1,300ft. Walking time: 4 hours.

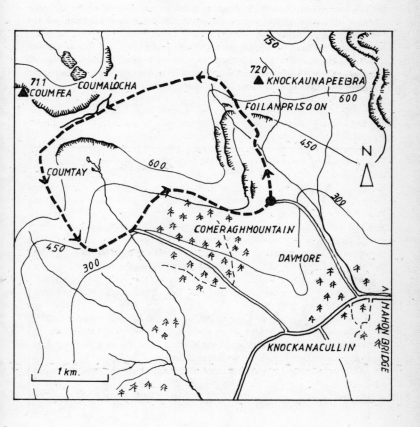

COUMFEA
711
COUMALOCHA
COUMTAY
COUMFEA

KNOCKAUNAPEEBRA
720
FOILANPRISOON
600
450
N
600
300
COMERAGHMOUNTAIN
DAVMORE
450
300
KNOCKANACULLIN
MAHON BRIDGE
1 km.

Reference OS Map: Sheet 22 (1:126,720).

43. CROHAUN

The little cone of Crohaun 482m/1,591ft, stands alone just south of the main Comeragh range. It is separated from Farbreaga by a broad col. A very scenic road runs through it (from Lemybrien to Kilbrien) which rises to around 340m/1,150ft at its highest point.

From Dungarvan take the N25 to Lemybrien. Follow the signs for 'Comeragh Drive' on roads heading west or northwest. Cross Dalligan bridge and park at the top of the road 270 016 a few hundred metres beyond a large layby.

The views from here are superb — Dungarvan town, the Bay of Helvick Head to the south; the sandy beaches and cliffs from Tramore round to Youghal seem almost beneath your feet. The Comeragh Mountains stretch northwards through the heart of Co. Waterford.

Distance: 2.4km/1.5miles. Ascent: 150m/500ft. Walking time: 1 hour.

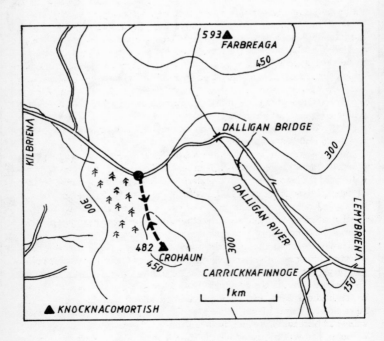

Reference OS Map: Sheet 22 (1:126,720).

44. CIRCUIT OF THE NIRE VALLEY

From Clonmel take the R671 south to Ballymacarbry. Drive eastwards along the valley of the Nire River towards the Nire church. Pass the church and carry on to the large layby above the river, 278 126.

From your starting point you can see clearly (on a fine day) the outline of your day's walk — Coumfea the westernmost coum, the Coumalochas, the Sgilloge Loughs and Coumlara, all north-facing coums and all except the last one containing attractive little lakes.

The word Comeragh comes from 'Cumarach' which means full of hollows, glacial in origin. Indeed the majority of Comeragh names incorporate coum (hollow or valley) in some form. The main tributary of the Nire (*Nier*) rises from the most easterly of them — the Sgilloge Loughs and is joined by other streams. The Nire itself rises from the central group, the Coumalochas and to the west is one more, the highest, the deepest and the largest, Coumfea.

The layby is a very popular place in summer. It overlooks the Nire Valley and is an ideal spot from which to explore these mountains.

From the carpark follow the signs for the 'Nire Lakes' (yellow) along a path keeping close to a stone wall and tiny stream. Go through a small timber gate, down close to a farmhouse sheltered by coniferous trees. A prehistoric standing stone is just above you to the left. Continue along the edge of the trees, past a sheep-pen to another timber gate. You are now out on to open ground. Turn sharply right along a wall dropping down to the river. (There are yellow markings on stones to mark the path, some of which is eroded just above the river.)

N.B. The river itself can sometimes be difficult to cross in winter, especially after a spell of rain.

After crossing the river head in a southwest direction to the long spur which is the western arm of Coumfea. Walking this area can be a bit tedious as the terrain is marshy underfoot and as well as the upper course of the Nire itself there are a few small streams to cross. However, you will be rewarded by spectacular views of the coums on your left with their sheer precipices dropping down to the lakes which are the special splendour of the Comeraghs.

Having reached the spur the route continues uphill in a southeast direction along a gentle grassy slope. The cliffs of Coumfea are just below you on the left. A tiny cairn marks the summit of Coumfea 711m/2,340ft.

You are now on the relatively featureless plateau of the Comeraghs, which in these parts offers some pleasant walking and fine views — the lakes nearly 300m/1,000ft below, the Gap, the Knockanaffrin ridge, the valleys of Nire and Lyre and, in the distance, other mountains.

Soon, you will be just above the coum containing the Sgilloge Loughs, beside a little stream which plunges steeply over rocks unto the inner lake below. The northwest winds blow the spray back upwards along cliffs (known as *Sean Bhean ag caitheamh tobac*, Old Woman Smoking a Pipe) which in winter freezes into weirdly shaped icicles on the vegetation and rocks.

About 100m/yds of uphill walking will take you to 731m/2,400ft and the head of Coumlara (not named on ½ inch map). This valley is narrow and, on its western side, steep. It contains a sparkling stream which runs busily down the first few hundred metres and then meanders gently as the valley floor levels out towards the Gap.

Descend by the middle of the valley over ferns and mosses, keeping the river on your left. Alternatively, if you are fortunate enough you will pick up a contouring sheep track on the eastern slope which will take you all the way to the Gap.

At the Gap you now have a choice — of continuing the circuit by taking in Knockanaffrin or returning directly to the layby. If you decide on the latter, follow the white stakes out to the layby in order to avoid the marshy ground lower down.

If you decide on taking in Knockanaffrin you can look forward to enjoying some very pleasant, easy walking up along the ridge. You will be surprised how quickly you will gain height.

After approximately 45 minutes and about 300m/1,000ft of ascent you will be on top at 753m/2,478ft.

Descend by retracing your steps to the cliffs above L. Coumduala. From here walk in a southwest direction along the spur which drops down directly to the layby.

Distance: 18km/11miles. Ascent: 820m/2,700ft. Walking time: 6½ hours.

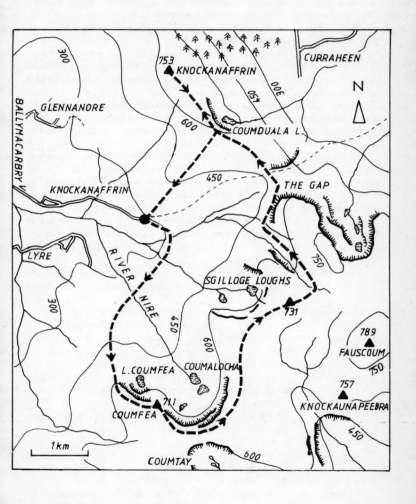

Reference OS Map: Sheet 22 (1:126,720).

45. SEEFIN AND FARBREAGA HORSESHOE

The Monavullagh mountains, of which Seefin is the highest point, are a continuation of and very similar to the Comeraghs. The name 'Monavullagh' itself means 'Turf at the top of a hill'. In fact the valleys are much drier and the tops far less boggy than the Comeraghs.

The circuit of the Araglin valley is a very pleasant walk with many spectacular views of mountain and coastline and is an easy route from a navigational point of view.

Approximately 15km/9miles northwest of Dungarvan on the R672 you will come to a crossroads with a filling station on your left. Take a right turn for Kilbrien. After 2.8km/1.8miles you will come to Scart Bridge (Sawmills). Cross the bridge and after about 30m/yds turn right. Immediately before Kilbrien village you will see a school on your left. Turn left after the school and travel 1.7km/1.1miles along this road to another road on your left. Take this road for 2km/1.25miles approx., to a sharp left turn — 258 050. Park here. (The road on your right is not marked on some ½ inch OS maps.)

Cross the fence and walk northwards close to a stone wall and the edge of a forest. Cross another fence and continue with the forest on your right (there are signs of an old track along the forest edge) to the boundary between an old and a young forest. Walk uphill along the track at the edge of the young forest through a double wooden gate to just below point 367m/1,204ft. Turn right and ascend along a track all the way to the summit of Seefin 725m/2,387ft.

The first thing you notice is the ugly manmade structure built for the purpose of providing multi-channel TV for places along the south coast of Ireland.

The summit of Seefin provides some of the finest and most extensive views of the Waterford coastline, including Dungarvan Bay and Helvick Head; the Comeragh plateau to the north and the Galtees and Knockmealdowns in the distance.

Descend southwards for about 220m/700ft along a wire fence to the Barnamadra gap (Dog's gap) in the heart of the Monavullaghs. Here there is to be seen a standing stone and stone circle of pre-historic origin in the middle of the col.

The legendary St Declan's path went from Kilbrien and the Araglin valley through Barnamadra to Mahon Bridge and Kilmacthomas on the eastern side.

The fence continues up the opposite hillside to 610m/2,000ft from where the necessary direction is almost due south across a marshy plateau to Farbreaga (*Fear Breaga*, False Man: 593m/1,953ft).

Descend north-westwards for about 120m/yds. Then contour northwards to just below the gap. Here you will just about discern the old track of St Declan's path if you look up towards the gap on your right.

Make for the ruins of an old farm building with a rusty roof among a small V-shaped cluster of coniferous trees. Cross the stream, then pass through a gate where you will pick up the track which completes the horseshoe.

Distance: 11km/7miles. Ascent: 610m/2,000ft. Walking time: 4½ hours.

B. Alternative Route

Seefin Mountain itself is a peak which is reached almost entirely on tracks so it can be enjoyed by people without navigational skills, if after reaching the peak they descend by retracing their steps.

Distance: 7km/4.5miles. Ascent: 460m/1,500ft. Walking time: 3 hours.

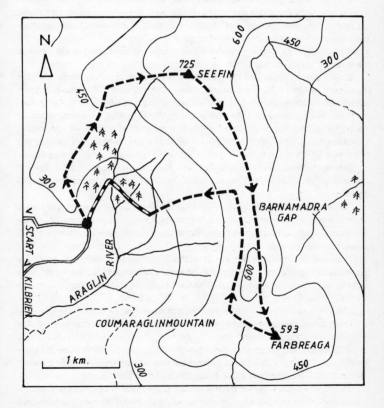

Reference OS Map: Sheet 22 (1:126,720).

This long distance walk, organised by the Peaks Climbing Club, is held every year in April. It starts from the top of the road 270 016 southwest of Dalligan Bridge and extends northwards from Farbreaga in the Monavullaghs over the Comeragh plateau to the Gap, along the Knockanaffrin ridge and ending at Powers the Pot 256 197.

The Comeraghs have a reputation for their bogginess but the route takes in the drier sections, which makes for pleasant walking and some fine views along the way.

Fred Carew, an enthusiastic walker all his life, was the first president of the Peaks club, until his death in 1985.

To get to the start of the walk, head for Lemybrien a small village where the N25 joins the R676. Roads leading west from here and sign-posted 'Comeragh Drive' will take you to the col between Crohaun and Farbreaga. There is ample parking here.

Walk northwards along a gentle spur, then eastwards towards Farbreaga itself 593m/1,953ft. Continue towards the broad grassy spur of the unnamed top 610m/2,000ft and descend along a wire fence to the Barnamadra Gap. There are about 200m/650ft of uphill to Seefin 725m/2,387ft, fairly steep at first but levelling off towards the summit.

From Seefin the route descends along the Comeragh plateau and up an almost unnoticeable 60m/200ft to the edge of the cliffs of Coumtay. Continue across land to the broad upper course of the Mahon River where you have to drop 120m/400ft and cross the river itself before rising again to the top of the twin-cairned cone of Knockaunapeebra 726m/2,384ft (Hillock of the Piper). It is worth taking a short break here to take in the fine views.

Fauscoum at 789m/2,597ft is the highest point in the Comeraghs but it is an insignificant summit on top of an elevated bog and can be easily missed in poor weather conditions. So, in those circumstances it is prudent to take a bearing from Knockaunapeebra to the top of the narrow valley north of east of the Sgilloge Loughs. This enables the walker to cross an intricate section of the Comeragh plateau on one bearing. This route also has the advantage of avoiding the 'blackest bog' of the plateau!

Take care to enter this valley on the right-hand side and follow the right-hand side of the river as you descend towards the Gap.

The top of the Knockanaffrin Ridge is almost 300m/yds from here but it offers the most pleasant walking of the entire route. Continue from 753m/2,478ft, the highest point, to the trig. point on top of Knock-sheegowna, 679m/2,181ft (not named on the ½ inch OS), your final peak of the day. The finish is now in sight. It is the line of coniferous trees about 4km/2.5miles to the northwest. Coming off 664m/2,181ft, walkers who keep to the following suggestions will be rewarded by the driest line available. Descend northwest along the spur, keeping well above the river until you are in line with the buildings of Powers the Pot. Then, veer directly west, cross the stream and walk through a green field to the finish.

N.B. It is important to be aware that there is a substantial road journey between the start and the finish of this long-distance walk.

Distance: 25km/15.5miles. Ascent: 850m/2,800ft. Walking time: 7/9 hours.

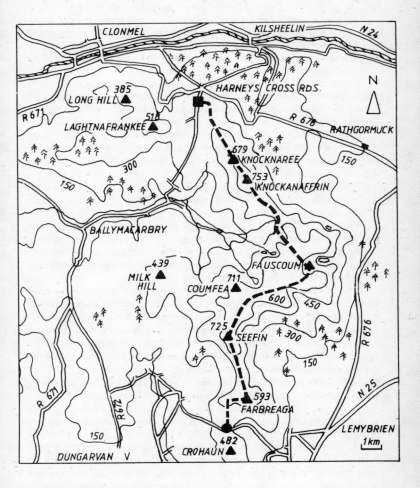

Reference OS Map: Sheet 22 (1:126,720).

47. KNOCKMEALDOWN-SUGARLOAF HORSESHOE

The Clogheen-Lismore road, R668, is one of the most scenic drives in the southeast. From Clogheen the road winds up through steep woods as far as the Vee Gap and continues southwards across moorland with superb views. The Grubb monument is about 150m/yds beyond the hairpin bend opposite the sign for 'Premier Drive'. This tombstone marks the grave of Samuel Grubb who had lived and owned property in the Golden Vale and wished to be buried in sight of his paradise. According to a local tale, he gave orders to be buried on the very top of the hills but six strong bearers could go no further — he would see no better on top!

Continuing along the road you come to Bay Lough on your right. It is a corrie lake, dammed by morainic deposits. It is reputed to be bottomless and inhabited by the ghost of 'Petticoat Loose'. In summer it is surrounded by a magnificent display of rhododendrons. The old road used to go straight up the valley past the Bay Lough. It is still walkable. The Sugar Loaf and Knockmealdowns are on your left.

Just before the junction with the Cappoquin road (R669) you can park your car in the car park on the right, across the road from some trees which hide a derelict house 039 079.

Proceed uphill along a gentle slope with patches of short heather until you reach the summit of *Cnoc Maol Donn* (Bare Brown Mountain: 793m/2,609ft).

For those walkers who do not have time to continue the route you may now retrace your steps to your car.

Lismore and Cappoquin lie at the foot of the ridge while the south coast can be made out in the distance. On very clear winter days sightings of the Kerry mountains have been reported.

It is said that this was the spot chosen for burial by Major Eeles of Lismore who wrote extensively in the eighteenth century on the use of electricity as a cure for mental illness. There are no traces of his grave, however.

Descend in a north-westerly direction over short springy heather, again along the wall to a col. Ascend the final 90m/300ft of the day to the summit of Sugar Loaf 653m/2,144ft, a double cairned peak overlooking the broad plains of Tipperary.

This section from Knockmealdown to Sugar Loaf is the most spectacular part of the walk. The ridge is at its narrowest and the views are superb.

From Sugar Loaf descend steeply, following a low wall to the large layby at the highest point of the Vee Gap.

The shelter at the top of the road marks the spot where Bianconi's tired stage coach horses were changed after the long haul up from the valley below. At the layby also, there is an altar where Mass is celebrated every year.

Return to the car by walking along the road.

Knockmealdown Mountain
Distance: 5km/3miles. Ascent: 520m/1,700ft. Walking time: 2½ hours.

Horseshoe
Distance: 10km/6miles. Ascent: 600m/2,000ft. Walking time: 3½/4 hours.

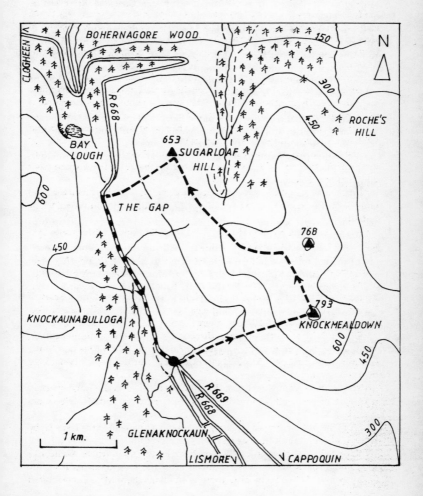

Reference OS Map: Sheet 22 (1:126,720).

48. KNOCKMEALDOWN FROM THE NORTHERN VALLEYS

↑

This is one of the most interesting walks in this range. To gain maximum enjoyment from it, park a car at the finish, known locally as the 'Meeting of the Waters'. It is the confluence of the Glengalla River and a tributary at 077 111.

The walk begins at the hairpin bend 042 118 on the way up to the Vee Gap (on the R668 south of Clogheen). There is plenty of space for parking. From this point at about 250m/800ft you can see Clogheen Village beneath you to the northwest and the Comeragh Gap to the east. The Galty Mountains are slightly west of north. Castlegrace, home of the Grubb family, is in the valley slightly west of north. On a clear day you can see the Devil's Bit in the distant north.

Leave the road at the very point of the hairpin bend. Proceed northeast along various tracks dropping down towards the stream until you meet a good wide path about 50m/170ft above the stream.

Follow this path south to the head of the valley where you bear left along the top edge of the wood (the tiny Lough Moylan is now dried up and surrounded by trees).

After about seven minutes there is a broad easy gully on your right. Climb this gully southwest to the main ridge. Follow the earth ditch (at this point along the county bounds of Waterford and Tipperary) to the top of Knockmealdown 793m/2,609ft.

Descend steeply over easy ground towards a wide col. From the east side of the col follow a faint track east of north leading to a corner of a new wood (within eight minutes). Contour along the eastern edge of a new unmapped wood and take the third rough track downwards. You will cross another path on your way down to the edge of a minor stream. Continue along this track until you pick up a rough road running north on the east bank of the main stream.

This area has several contouring forest roads but the route described will keep you on a line approximating the one shown on the ½ inch map which leads directly to the Meeting of the Waters.

Distance: 11km/7miles. Ascent: 550m/1,800ft. Walking time: 4 hours.

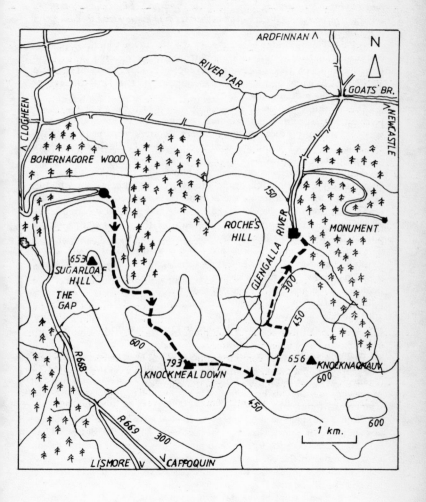

49. THE EASTERN KNOCKMEALDOWNS

(From the Liam Lynch Monument to the Vee Gap)

This traverse over easy terrain takes in most of the major peaks of the range and is an exhilarating walk. The ridge forms part of the boundary between counties Tipperary and Waterford and contrasts dramatically with the lush farms of the lowlands.

Drive to Goat's Bridge (*Goatenbridge*) 087 136 on the Clogheen to Newcastle road and turn south along a narrow road signposted to the Liam Lynch Monument. This road leads on to a forest road with several junctions all of which have signposts to the monument. Park just before the entrance to the monument at 007 112.

This monument, a small round tower for which the stone was gathered off the surrounding mountains, commemorates Liam Lynch who was commanding officer of the southern Republicans during the Civil War. He was shot down on the mountain side near Goatenbridge in April 1923 just before the ceasefire.

Above the monument on the lower slopes of Crohan West there is a young forest plantation. It is prudent to keep to the firebreak a few metres right of the tower just inside the entrance gate and follow it and a wire fence to the top of Crohan West. Pause, now and then, to absorb the fine views unfolding all around you. (Because of the rough nature of the terrain, this route is easier to ascend than descend.)

Drop down along a wall to a col and ascend gradually over grassy terrain to Knockmeal 562m/1,846ft. Descend to the southwest along a wall after Knockmeal towards the corner of a new wood. Here, you veer away from the ditch and proceed upwards to the broad summit of Knocknafallia 670m/2,199ft — a strenuous ascent but you will be rewarded by splendid views from the large cairn which marks the summit. Care and precision are required to find this cairn in mist as it is off the centre of the plateau.

From here you will be able to see the southern side of the ridge for the first time — the River Blackwater meandering southwards towards Youghal Bay, the large grey buildings of Mount Melleray, a Cistercian Monastery on the lower slopes of Knocknafallia, and eastwards the Comeragh Mountains.

From Knocknafallia the route now crosses a col and on to the stone-strewn ridge of Knocknagav (*Conc na gCnabh*, Hill of the Bones: 649m/ 2,132ft). Here you pick up the wall again with its small summit cairns. Descend now to the col just under Knockmealdown. An ancient ecclesiastical route from Cashel to Ardmore passed through this col, traces of which are still discernible.

The biggest ascent of the day now awaits you! — with Knockmealdown looming up ahead. It is 300m/1,000ft from here to the top of the highest peak in the range, Knockmealdown itself (*Cnoc Maol Donn*, Bare

Brown Mountain 793m/2,609ft). Follow the wall, which goes steeply to the top where you will be rewarded by excellent views and the knowledge that your day's work is almost done.

The rest of the walk over the Sugarloaf to the Vee Gap is the same as Walk 47.

Distance: 14km/5miles. Ascent: 1,000m/3,300ft. Walking time: 6 hours.

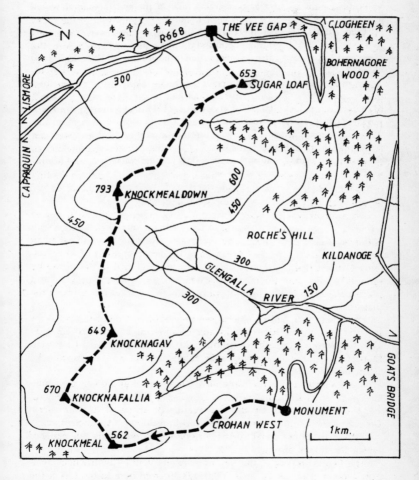

Reference OS Map: Sheet 22 (1:126,720).

50. THE WESTERN KNOCKMEALDOWNS

This route, together with the eastern Knockmealdowns, can be linked to make up a full traverse of the range.

From the Vee Gap 031 100 (at the highest point on the R668 between Clogheen and Lismore) walk uphill to an unnamed peak at 610m/2,000ft. A faint path through the heather makes this steep ascent a little easier. As you gain height be sure to pause and take in the spectacular views all around.

From 610m/2,000ft drop 60m/200ft south-westwards over easy terrain to a long col. Then head in a northwest direction and up 90m/300ft to the large and impressive cairn of Knockshanahullion, Hill of the Old Elbow: 654m/2,153ft.

From Knockshanahullion descend southwest along a broad spur to a minor road which goes through the col just under Farbreaga. This hill, 517m/1,706ft, is just 90m/300ft above the col. From Farbreaga head in a north-westerly direction to a rough track (marked on ½ inch map) just west of the main stream. Follow it through a gate and on to a surfaced road and Kilcaroon Bridge 951 131.

Distance: 12km/7.5miles. Ascent: 460m/1,500ft. Walking time: 4 hours.

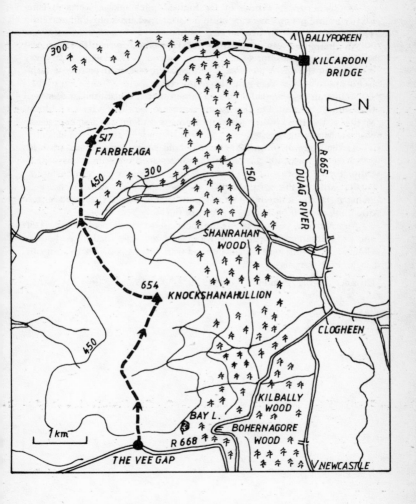

300

BALLYPOREEN

KILCAROON
BRIDGE

N

517
FARBREAGA

450

300

150

R 665

DUAG RIVER

SHANRAHAN
WOOD

654
KNOCKSHANAHULLION

CLOGHEEN

450

BAY L.

R 668

KILBALLY
WOOD

BOHERNAGORE
WOOD

1 km

THE VEE GAP

NEWCASTLE

Reference OS Map: Sheet 22 (1:126,720).

131

51. KNOCKNAFALLIA FROM MOUNT MELLERAY

Travelling north on the R669 from Cappoquin (on the Clogheen Rd) take the second turning right, then left through the main gates of the abbey.

At the northwest corner of the football pitch take a series of laneways running north, emerging on to moorland where there is a large Holy Year cross.

An alternative way of reaching the cross is to drive up the road past the monastery gates for exactly 0.5 miles and park. Follow a laneway (marked on the OS ½ inch map) to the northwest until you see a farmhouse ahead of you. Veer right, up to the cross.

Follow an easy angled spur to a large cairn at the southeast corner of the summit plateau. On the ascent there are excellent views of Mount Melleray, the Blackwater, Knockmealdowns and in the distance, to the east, the Monavullaghs.

At the summit, 670m/2,199ft, a whole new world opens up with extensive views of all the mountain ranges in the southeast as well as Dungarvan Bay.

Onwards to the col under Knockmeal. Here you have a choice — swing right and following a stoney path at the edge of the wood largely downhill, contour back to the vicinity of the Holy Year cross.

Alternatively, you can tackle the short rise to Knockmeal 563m/1,846ft and drop down eastwards to the Melleray-Newcastle road at the head of Glennafallia. From here a pleasant road walk brings you back to your car.

For both options—

Distance: 12km/7.5miles. Ascent: 550m/1,800ft. Walking time: 4½ hours.

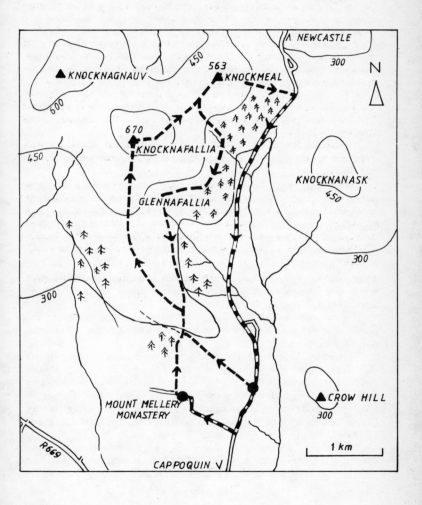

Reference OS Map: Sheet 22 (1:126,720).

133

THE EAST MUNSTER WAY

The East Munster Way is a low-level way-marked route following tow-paths, old tracks, forest roads, country roads and occasionally open moorland. It is linked to the South Leinster Way and there are plans to connect it with the Kerry Way.

The OS map no. 22 (½ inch to 1 mile) covers the area of the trail but its route is not marked. It is, however, marked on the 1:250,000 OS no. 4. It begins in Carrick-on-Suir and heads mainly west across south Tipperary and north Waterford to the Vee above Clogheen. Strong walkers can easily reach the Vee in two days using Clonmel as an overnight stop.

52. THE EAST MUNSTER WAY: CARRICK-ON-SUIR TO CLONMEL

An old towpath by the River Suir is used along this tranquil stretch between the two busy towns of Carrick and Clonmel.

The path was built in the late eighteenth century for the horses that pulled flat-bottomed boats laden with raw materials for the industries of Clonmel. Nowadays it is hard to imagine it was once the main highway of Co. Tipperary.

The starting point for the day's walk is the Suir towpath at the Quays in Carrick. There are so many things to be seen along this stretch of the river — many fine towerhouses, traditional fishing cots, old boat houses, great varieties of wild flowers and wild life. There are, constantly, great splashes and sounds on the river itself, the moorhen, the duck and the leaping trout disturbing the calm waters.

The route leads directly along the towpath to the bridge in the picturesque village of Kilsheelan, a perfect place to pause for a while and quench your thirst.

Thus rested, cross Kilsheelan bridge and enter Gurteen wood by the old Alms house, now a private residence. The climbing track follows forest roads out of the Suir Valley with the eminence of Slievenamon framing the distant view across the rich fertile valley below. Further on there are splendid views of the Knockanaffrin ridge, the Comeragh corries in the distance and, to the west and a little closer, Laghtnafrankee and Long Hill.

The route joins a public road at Harney's Cross and from here you drop down to rejoin the towpath at Sir Thomas Bridge for the short stretch to Clonmel ending near Lady Blessington's Bath.

Distance: 30.5km/19miles. Ascent: 300m/1,000ft. Walking time: 7/9 hours.

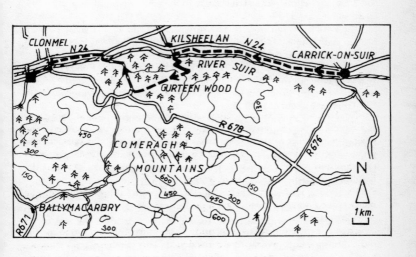

Reference OS Map: Sheet 22 (1:126,720).

135

53. THE EAST MUNSTER WAY: CLONMEL TO THE VEE

The starting point for this stage of the route is just south of the Old Bridge in Clonmel. Proceed to Roaring Spring road, where you veer left up a steep country road, from where markers lead you to the Holy Year cross. This point is a prominent landmark above Clonmel and an excellent place to pause awhile and absorb the beauty of your surroundings.

From here the route veers westwards for a while before joining a very old road which is followed southwards. This road bypasses the old deserted village of Glenary and leads to a ford on the Glenary River, 204 191, which is crossed to reach a forest trail leading up to a forest road where you turn right, crossing a concrete bridge. Then, turn left at two junctions, still climbing to swing away to the southwest corner of Russellstown state forest 178 169.

The Way turns left from Russellstown Forest, then forks right, down a boreen with almost as much grass as tarmac, while ahead is a splendid panorama of the Knockmealdown Mountains.

After crossing the busy R671 (Clonmel to Dungarvan Road) the way winds mainly southwest leaving Four Mile Water Catholic Church on the left, crossing first Four Mile Water Bridge, then Creggane Bridge, to enter Co. Tipperary again at 162 133.

Then the village of Newcastle is reached and once again, the banks of the River Suir, passing Bannard House on the right; from Newcastle, the Mount Melleray road is taken for some 5km/3miles. Then, look for an old track on the right, cut off from tarmac by a low stone wall (113 104). This track links with a forest road and, where a left turn leads west, passes the modern round tower monument to Liam Lynch killed in the Civil War 1922–23. From here the majestic outline of the Galty mountains enhances the beauty of the surrounding landscape.

Zig-zagging down, the forest road crosses a path on the site of an ancient trackway called Rian Bo Phadraig — 'The track of St Patrick's cow' — which linked Lismore to Ardfinnan and Cashel, passing over the mountains through the col just under their highest point (Knockmealdown itself).

The Munster Way crosses a bridge over the Glengalla stream; then it leaves a waterworks installation on the left before reaching the tarmac 050 131, on the mountain foot road from Clogheen to Newcastle.

Turn left, on this road, then go left again, back into the forest, 2km/ 1.25miles further west, thus reaching the end of the stage at Loughnan's Bridge below the Vee 027 114.

Distance: 34km/21miles. Ascent: 910m/3,000ft. Walking time: 9½/11½ hours.

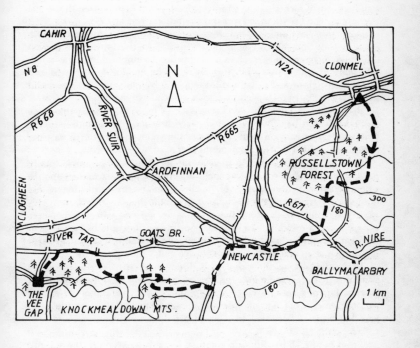

Reference OS Map: Sheet 22 (1:126,720).

Driving east from Kilbeheny on the N8 take the 2nd road on the left. After about 2km/1.25miles you will pass a pumphouse and just beyond this the road forks and you should take the right option. There is ample parking at the end of the tarred section of the road, near the corner of the wood 868 197.

Here you are at an elevation of over 300m/1,000ft and a clear day will enable you to enjoy the splendid views in all directions — particularly scenic and including my favourite section of the Galtees with long deep valleys from which rise the grassy sloped peaks. The lower slopes are densely forested (with many forest roads not marked on OS maps).

After you have lingered awhile admiring the peaks you should walk straight ahead for 400m/yds on a dirt road. Take the 1st gate on the left and follow a contouring track to the ruins of a farmhouse. From here, it is advisable to take a sharp left turn in order to avoid a deep ravine and other obstructions and go straight down (southwest) through three small fields. This brings you to a cart track on the banks of the Behanagh River.

Proceed north along this track, cross a bridge, go through double gates and take the left-hand valley in a westerly direction. The going is easier if you keep the stream on your left. Soon, the valley swings north past the curious outcrop of Pigeon Rock on the slopes of Knocknascrow.

This is a delightful little place with its interlocking spurs, totally cutting off all views except the enclosing mountains — a perfect spot to rest and listen to the sounds of the birds and sheep who inhabit this wilderness paradise by the rushing waters of the Pigeon Rock River.

Just beyond Pigeon Rock the slope eases and you can now begin to ascend along a minor stream bed in a northwest direction. Now, views of Knockaterriff and beyond, the summit cone of Galtymore, unfold. The top of the ridge is soon reached, giving extensive valley views in all directions.

Proceeding along the ridge in a direction west of north, the great summit cairn of Temple Hill is soon reached, 786m/2,579ft. Descending eastwards from Temple Hill, swing slightly south to avoid the gullies running into the Glen of Aherlow. After reaching the Temple Hill-Knockaterriff col, proceed in a northeast direction to the col south of Lyracappul.

From here a short climb up a grassy slope brings you to the summit rocks of Lyracappul (Confluence of the Horse: 827m/2,712ft). Now follow the wall for about 1km/0.5miles and take a sharp turn in the direction just east of south towards Monabrack 610m/2,000ft.

Time to pause again and view the evidence of turf cutting in the past, much of it for burning in the local creameries. To the northwest, there are further cuttings at 670m/2,200ft between Lyracappul and Knockaterriff, and a path to the area can still be discerned. Horse sleighs used to bring out the turf over the grassy terrain can still be found in local barns.

A short rise will take you to the broad summit plateau of Monabrack. Descending from here and heading south you will soon cross a fence from where you should be able to pick out your vehicle ahead of you.

Make for the right-hand side of the small clump of trees, and from here a cart track leads you directly back to your starting point.

Distance: 14km/9miles. Ascent: 730m/2,400ft. Walking time: 5½ hours.

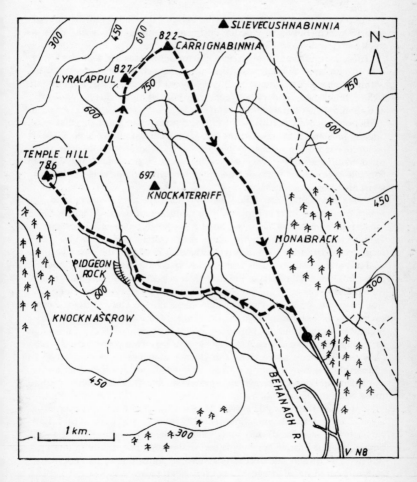

Reference OS Map: Sheet 22 (1:126,720).

55. GALTY WALL AND GALTYMORE

Travelling east from Kilbeheny on the N8 (Cahir to Mitchelstown Road), take the second turning on the left. After passing a pumphouse (2km/1.25miles) the road forks and you should take the narrow left option. Keep an eye out for a bridge; just before reaching it there is parking for about two cars. If required, there is further parking a few hundred metres/yds beyond the bridge, 864 196.

Follow a cart track north along the bank of the Behanagh River. Proceed 150m/yds beyond a wooden bridge and double gates, then follow a track and dry stone wall northwards.

These magnificent loose stone walls are an interesting feature of this area. A similar wall runs along the top of the ridge from Lyracappul to within approximately 60m/65yds of Galtymore. These walls, built about 1880, formed the boundary between the estates of the Buckleys, landlords of Galty Castle, and the Massey Estate.

Follow the wall northwards to its end and at the ruins of what was once a substantial farmhouse on the 1,300ft contour (OS Sheet No. 22) continue contouring for about 0.8km/0.5miles where you will again pick up a track descending very gently to where it crosses a ford with a concrete base. At the western side of the ford you will be able to pick out signs of old potato ridges.

After crossing the ford, follow a path of long zig-zags to where it finally peters out among turf cuttings. Continue in a northwest direction up a long spur. Eventually the slope eases and shortly afterwards you reach the wall along the top of the ridge. All your efforts are rewarded by spectacular views into the Glen of Aherlow and far beyond if the day is clear.

Follow the wall eastwards at first. Above Lake Curra it runs southeastwards. Above the cliffs of the corrie is a perfect place to rest and absorb the splendid views in all directions. Thus refreshed, continue along the wall to where it finally runs out and there is now only a short ascent eastwards to Galtymore 919m/3,018ft. Outside of Kerry, Galtymore is the highest point in Munster.

From Galtymore, the easiest way home is to retrace your steps as far as Dawsons Table, southwest of Lake Curra. From here you descend in a southerly direction aiming for a few isolated deciduous trees just to the north side of Monabrack wood. This would make an excellent site for those wishing to camp.

Just below the trees you should be able to cross the stream and follow a rough track into Monabrack wood. A forest road takes you south, right through the woodland, and eventually leads to a public tarred road. Follow this road for 150m/170yds taking the first gap on the right and go due west from here, down to your starting point, through a few fields, carefully avoiding any large areas of scrub and briar.

Distance: 16km/10miles. Ascent: 640m/2,100ft. Walking time: 5½ hours.

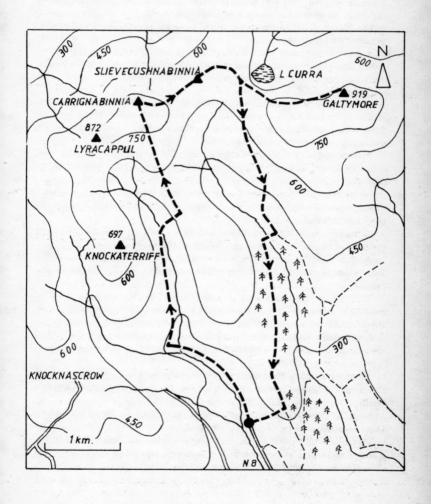

Reference OS Map: Sheet 22 (1:126,720).

141

56. GALTYMORE BY THE 'BLACK ROAD'

Galtymore is the highest peak in Munster outside of Co. Kerry and as such is the dominant feature of the landscape of north Munster. It is clearly visible from most main roads in south Tipperary but its twin peak profile is best seen from the N8 (the main Cahir-Mitchelstown Road).

The 'Black Road', an old turf track, rises to 640m/2,100ft just under Galtybeg and the main Galty ridge. The ease of access this gives makes the ascent of Galtymore the least demanding and one of the most popular Irish munros. In recent years Galtymore has tended to attract large numbers of walkers, especially on Sundays, but solitude is still to be found there during the week.

The approach is from the Mitchelstown to Cahir stretch of the N8. Coming from Mitchelstown, take the minor road on the left, 500m/0.3miles east of Skeheenarinky limestone schoolhouse. A disused pub a few metres beyond the corner will confirm the junction for you (907 175).

Drive straight up the minor road ignoring all forks, until you reach the end of the tarred section. Here you will find a small carpark on your right, 893 205.

Walk through two gates, taking care to close them after you, and follow the track known as the Black Road (shown on OS Sheet No. 22) to its end, immediately south of Galtybeg.

From here, walking in a north-western direction and rising gently, you will soon arrive at the col between Galtybeg and Galtymore.

As this is a sheltered spot with new views northwards towards the Glen of Aherlow and beyond, you are encouraged to rest awhile and have a snack.

Thus fortified you are well prepared to tackle the only hard work of the day's outing — the summit slopes of Galtymore. At the summit, 919m/3,018ft, you will find a discreet cross laboriously put in position by Ted Kevanagh and friends from Tipperary Town. You may also come across a plaque put there by the late Colonel Blake, who for many years organised an annual ascent of Galtymore on Whit Sunday.

From the summit descend first to the southwest and then along a broad spur in a southeast direction, aiming for the most northerly tip of Cooper's Wood.

Here, at the confluence of two streams is a most attractive little place to rest when the sun shines. When, finally, you have to press on, do so by following a rough path which heads uphill along the eastern side of the wood. Tracks in a southeastern direction will rejoin the Black Road just above the higher gate.

Distance: 10km/6miles. Ascent: 580m/1,900ft. Walking time: 4 hours.

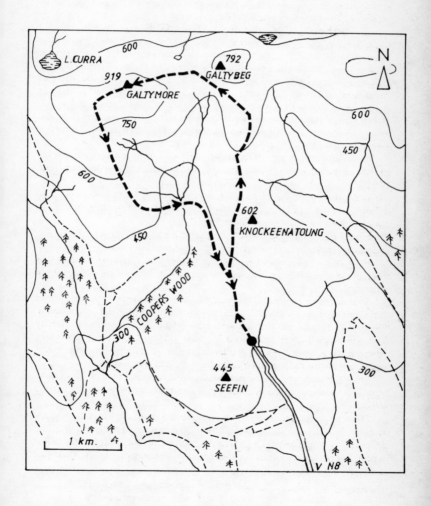

600
L. CURRA
792
▲ GALTYBEG
919
▲
GALTYMORE
750
600
450
600
450
602
▲
KNOCKEENATOUNG
300
COOPER'S WOOD
300
445
▲
SEEFIN
1 km.
N
△
V N8

Reference OS Map: Sheet 22 (1:126,720).

57. GALTYMORE, GALTYBEG, O'LOUGHNAN'S CASTLE FROM MOUNTAIN LODGE YOUTH HOSTEL

This route is very popular among hill walkers using Mountain Lodge youth hostel as a base. The hostel is situated deep in Glengara Wood 3km/2miles off the N8, 12.5km/8miles west of Cahir on the southern slopes of the Galtees. Occasionally in summer the wood gate maybe locked, in which case, you will have more opportunities to enjoy the grandeur of this wood by walking from its edge.

Glengara means Rough Glen and walkers not familiar with the wood are advised to keep to the path!

Starting from the main bridge near the youth hostel, 921 210, follow the forest road uphill on the east bank of the stream. This forest road after about 2km/1.25miles leads to the northwest corner of Glengara Wood. Leave the road at an extremely acute righthand bend where open ground is less than 50m/yds away.

Cross the first stream where the bank is low, at least 100m/yds from the corner of the wood. Continue in a westerly direction and cross another stream. Bearing northwest you should soon pick up traces of an old track going your way, eventually joining the Black Road at the col north of Knockeenatoung. Here you have joined the route to Galtymore described in Walk 56.

Follow the Black Road the short distance north to its end; then bear northwest, rising very slightly, and you will pick up a slightly worn path leading to the col between Galtybeg and Galtymore. A few hundred metres (about a thousand feet) below the col on the northern side is Lake Diheen (Tub) said to be inhabited by a snake banished there by St Patrick for eternity.

From the col your route rises sharply westwards to Galtymore, 919m/3,018ft, frequented by Spenser who called it 'Old Father Mole'.

After a short rest, retrace your steps towards Galtybeg and if you are thirsty keep an eagle eye open for the spring on the east slope of Galtymore. Having reached the col once again prepare for the short ascent of Galtybeg 792m/2,600ft. Here the ridge is at its narrowest and you can at once enjoy views on both north and south sides.

Continue eastwards to the next col and ascend the gradual slopes towards O'Loughnan's Castle, a rocky outcrop at the east end of a broad plateau. This particular spot offers excellent shelter and is a favourite place to rest and restore lost energy. A short stroll over to the edge of the cliffs will be rewarded by an excellent view of Lake Muskry. The outcrop itself is a clearly visible landmark from many of the roads to the north and southwest.

Bearing southwest will bring you to the northern edge of Glengara Wood where you are advised to enter the wood at the point of exit.

Distance: 14km/9miles. Ascent: 880m/2,900ft. Walking time: 5½ hours.

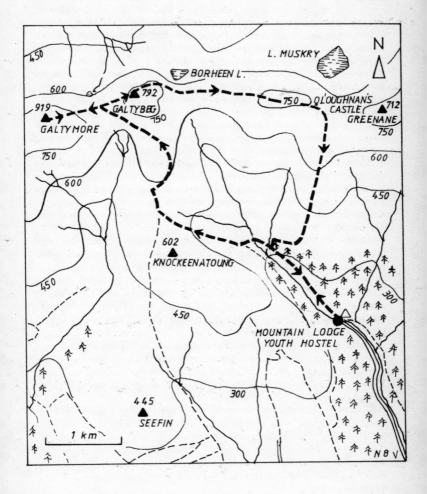

Reference OS Map: Sheet 22 (1:126,720).

58. GALTYMORE FROM THE GLENCUSH BOREEN

(Glen at the foot of the peak)

Even though this is a steep ascent it is the most popular and most direct route up Galtymore from the north side. It is the route followed when all and sundry climb the mountain on the organised annual climb on Whit Sunday.

All walks on the north side of the Galtees are approached from access points in the Glen of Aherlow. From Bansha, on the N24 Tipperary to Cahir road, take the road running southwest to Rossadrehid, 925 293 a tiny village due north of Lake Muskry. From Mitchelstown, take the R513 towards Limerick. After 10km/6miles turn right on the R662 and after 2.4km/1.5miles turn right again for about 18km/11miles towards Rossadrehid.

Driving west from Rossadrehid for 5.5km/3.5miles you reach the Clydagh Bridge 872 280. There is an unmarked tarred boreen running southwards on the east side of the stream. Car drivers are advised to drive only 1.2km/0.75miles up the wide section of this boreen where they will find parking at sheep pens on the right.

Walk to the end of the Glencush boreen. Follow a faint path across the moor to where it peters out after crossing a stream.

The moraine bank of Lake Diheen now confronts you and you should first head for the gully at its western end and then bear well right up the steep grassy slopes to the summit of Galtymore 919m/3,018ft. For those not accustomed to hill walking this is a far tougher and steeper route than the route on the Black Road from the south, described in Walk 56.

Having rested and enjoyed the views from the top, most will carefully retrace their steps backs to the start. If the weather is fine, some will be tempted by the less steep but slightly longer route down to Dawson's Table and follow the long easy spur to the north until almost in line with the top edge of Drumleagh Wood.

Now, you can gently drop down along the top edge of Drumleagh Wood and rejoin the end of the Glencush Boreen.

For Galtymore direct —
Distance: 8km/5miles. Ascent: 760m/2,500ft. Walking time: 4 hours.

For the route continuing around Lake Curra add half an hour to your time.

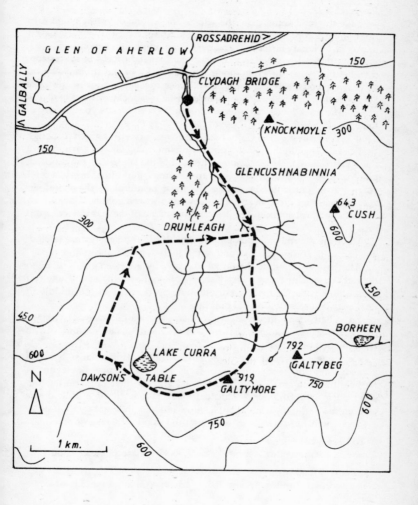

Reference OS Maps: Sheets 18 and 22 (1:126,720).

59. CIRCUIT OF LAKE MUSKRY

Leave the N24 (Cahir to Tipperary Road) at Bansha and take the road running southwest into the scenic Glen of Aherlow to the village of Rossadrehid 925 293.

Take the road south from the village and as you enter the wood turn right along a contouring forest road. Take the second turning left past a barrier (which may be locked) and park at a pumphouse beyond.

Walk through a wooden gate and take two right forks in succession, thus holding your direction along the west bank of the stream. As you leave the woods, a rising rough track gives excellent views of the Lake Muskry Cliffs topped by O'Loughnan's Castle — a rocky outcrop of glacial origin. The track levels out after a while and shortly leads you directly to Lake Muskry.

It is the largest of the Galty lakes and was formerly known as Lough Bel Sead (Lake with the Jewel Mouth, the name being taken from a story in the *Speckled Book of the MacEgans*). This told of the lake being the dwelling place of lovely maidens who were transformed into birds, every second year, one in particular becoming the most beautiful in the world. In keeping with her position she was allowed to wear a gold necklace which had a large jewel sparkling in it — and the name of the lake derives from this.

There are a number of possibilities now. If time and energy are limited, you can walk around the lake and return by the route you came.

Alternatively climb to the top of the ridge by the steep grassy slope to the right of the cliffs, after which a short walk to the southeast will take you to O'Loughnan's Castle, the curious outcrop perched in the middle of peat hags that resemble an old building.

From here, rising gently, make your way eastwards towards Greenane (*An Grianan*, The Summer Bower: 803m/2,636ft) a flat summit with a triangulation pillar.

Continue in a northeast direction for 1.5km/1mile across a broad plateau until you reach what is possibly a ruined booley. Booleying — farmers living in small stone shelters and grazing their cattle on the hill-sides during the summer — still took place here until the middle of the last century.

From here, head northwest and enter the woods at your exit point.

a) To Lake Muskry and back:
Distance: 10km/6miles. Ascent: 400m/1,300ft. Walking time: 3½ hours.

b) Circuit of the Corrie
Distance: 13km/8miles. Ascent: 760m/2,500ft. Walking time: 5 hours.

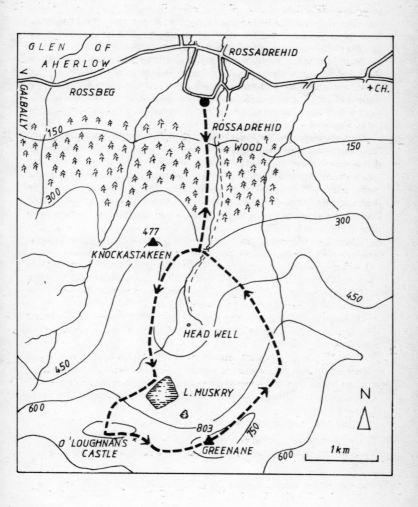

GLEN OF AHERLOW

GALBALLY

ROSSADREHID

ROSSBEG

ROSSADREHID WOOD

150

150

300

300

450

477

KNOCKASTAKEEN

HEAD WELL

450

600

L. MUSKRY

803

750

O'LOUGHNAN'S CASTLE

GREENANE

600

N

1km

Reference OS Maps: Sheets 18 and 22 (1:126,720).

60. GLENCUSH HORSESHOE

This is the most attractive and exhilarating walk in the Galtees, taking in views of all the Galty corries and lakes. For directions to starting point see instructions on access to the Clydagh Bridge (5.5km/3.5miles west of Rossadrehid) in Walk 58. Park at the bridge 872 280 and walk up the Glencush-nablinnia boreen (not marked on map) on the eastern side of the stream as far as the edge of the forest on your left (after about 1km/0.6miles).

From here head directly for Cush 643m/2,109ft. On its southern side a deep and sometimes boggy col is encountered on your way to Galtybeg 792m/2,600ft, the ice-sculptured northeast face of which is seen at its best from this angle of approach. Another more shallow col follows as you head west and begin the ascent of Galtymore keeping an eye open for the permanent spring on the way up.

On the summit itself, 919m/3,018ft, the tradition of having a cross has been continued. The present cross, a discreet metal one, was erected to replace a stone one damaged by storms.

Descending from Galtymore the route picks up the wall running along the ridge above Lake Curra. Leave the wall and head north along a broad spur, eventually taking the easy slopes towards the southwest corner of Drumleagh Wood in the distance. Shortly, you will pick up a ditch running north, which you follow over a prominent knoll to its end. Bearing right from here through a gate you will find a boreen leading down to the bridge.

Distance: 10km/6 miles. Ascent: 1,030m/3,400ft. Walking time: 5 hours.

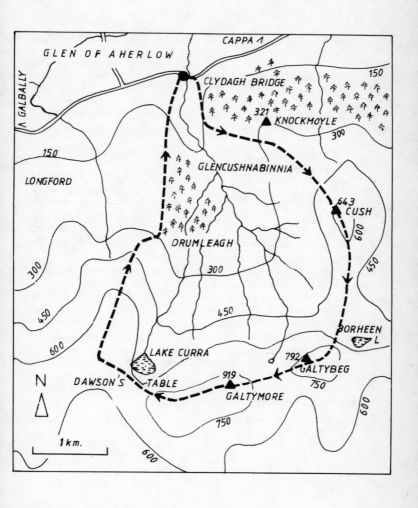

Reference OS Maps: Sheets 18 and 22 (1:126,720).

61. BALLYDAVID WOOD YOUTH HOSTEL TO MOUNTAIN LODGE YOUTH HOSTEL

This walk between the two Galty youth hostels is easily accomplished by seasoned walkers and though most of it is across the least interesting part of the ridge there are fine views.

From Ballydavid Wood Y.H. 977 283 in the Glen of Aherlow (2.5km/ 1.5miles east of Rossadrehid), follow the gravel road on long zig-zags to its end. Continue on a steep grassy track for a few hundred metres which brings you to the southwest corner of the wood marked on the ½ inch OS map. From here, along tracks and gaps in a new unmapped forest, follow as closely as you can a line southwest towards open moorland above you. Here, a note of warning! Between each double row of trees there are drains, many covered by long heather, conditions designed to punish the unwary.

Shortly after coming out on to the open moorland you will reach cairned Sturrakeen (Little Stump: 500m/1,650ft).

There is no trail as such even though there are occasional stone markers so far apart that they merely reassure you that you are on route rather than keep you on it.

From Sturrakeen continue southwest across boggy ground to a rocky outcrop above the 580m/1,900ft contour, and, holding the same direction, follow a slight rise to the cairn-surmounted peak which I take to be Laghtshanaquilla (Rocks of the Old Crock: 613m/2,010ft).

From it the route bears west and is defined now by traces of a ruined ditch which crosses numerous deep hags floored by a mixture of black peat and pink sandstone debris. Rise to what is probably a ruined booley at the eastern end of the Greenane plateau. The stone markers re-appear here taking you to the flat summit of Greenane (*An Grianan*, The Summer Bower: 803m/2,636ft) and along this stretch you have before you a superb view of Galtymore dominated by the ridge.

From Greenane, the most direct route is a line just west of south towards the northeast corner of Glengara Wood. From this corner go west for 600m/0.4miles and pick up a grassy firebreak leading to a forest road where you turn left and go directly down to the hostel.

Distance: 11km/6.8miles. Ascent: 760m/2,500ft. Walking time: 4½ hours.

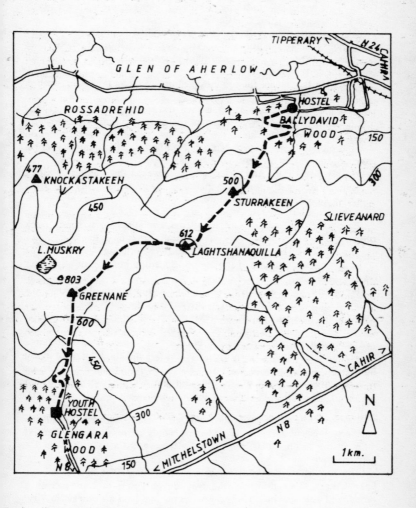

Reference OS Maps: Sheets 18 and 22 (1:126,720).

62. GALTY RIDGE WALK

The traverse of the Galty mountains is about 26km/16miles long and runs roughly east-west, ending or beginning in the historical town of Cahir. It is a superb ridge walk which includes 6 peaks over 650m/2,150ft and its highest peak, Galtymore 919m/3,018ft is one of the few Irish munros.

It is a demanding walk and the eastern third requires very precise navigation in misty conditions. It doesn't matter which direction one takes but I prefer to start at the western end to get the ascent of Temple Hill behind me early in the day.

However, that means the roughest ground and least interesting section is left until the evening.

Take the N8 north from Mitchelstown and just past Kilbeheny take the first road on your left. Drive to where there are two white-washed farm buildings, one on either side of the road. Then, 100m/yds or so further on at a sharp bend there is a wooden gate leading to a grassy track. There is parking for only one car here, 857 195.

Walk up this track and along a fence towards the southern spur of Temple Hill. (Note, that on the ½ inch map the exact position of the river is not registered correctly, so the track is shown on the wrong side of the river. In actual fact, the river is to the north of the track.)

Along the route you may come across a relatively new rough track running in your direction. This goes to within 70m/yds of the top.

The summit of Temple Hill, 786m/2,579ft, is dominated by a very large and impressive cairn, one of the many prehistoric burial grounds found on Irish peaks.

From here descend eastwards for 180m/600ft, over small boulders to a col, then northeast for 60m/200ft to another col between Knockaterriff and Lyracappul. This area requires careful navigation to avoid dropping too low below the first or second cols. In recent years this part of the Galtees has been explored in search of gold but efforts so far have yielded nothing.

The route continues upwards to Lyracappul and the little cairn at the top, 827m/2,712ft. A high stone wall runs from this point and it can be followed along the crest of the ridge for the next four miles to within 60m/200ft of Galtymore, passing the summit cairns of Carrignabinnia, 822m/2,697ft, and Slievecushnabinnia, 777m/2,549ft, along the way. The wall passes close to the cliffs above Lough Curra — a corrie lake on the northern slopes of the ridge. From here it is only 20 minutes to the highest point in the southeast of Ireland — Galtymore, 919m/3,018ft — and a superb viewpoint.

The route now descends westwards for 200m/700ft to a col above Lake Diheen. Two thirds of the way down you will come across a permanent spring which is a very welcome sight on an otherwise 'dry' route. Then a gradual ascent towards Galtybeg, from where you again drop down to another col with Lake Borheen beneath it to the north.

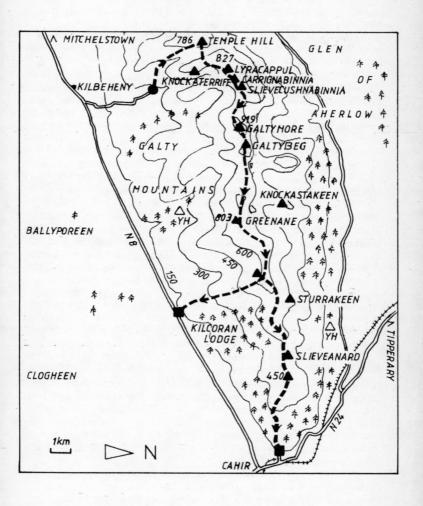

Reference OS Maps: Sheets 18 and 22 (1:126,720).

The route now crosses a plateau area towards the outcrop known as O'Loughnan's castle. This is a rather featureless and peaty section and, in mist, care should be taken to avoid dropping too low on the south side.

O'Loughnan's castle is a rocky outcrop sculptured by frost shattering during glacial times. Below it to the north is the largest and most attractive of the corrie lakes — Lake Muskry.

A short walk through peat hags and stoney ground takes you to the Greenane trig. point at 803m/2,636ft. Crossing the plateau in a northwest direction you will encounter occasional small cairns until you come to the end of the plateau known as Greenane-east. This can be identified by the presence of a ruined shelter and it marks an important directional change. From the col, follow a low earth bank running east through a series of deep peat hags until you reach the cairn north of 613m/2,010ft. This cairn marks the change in direction to the next col and peak, 579m/1,900ft. This is a broad col with a small outcrop. (Walkers heading for the Ballydavid Wood Y.H. should go northeast along the spur towards 503m/1,650ft.)

For those continuing to Cahir, continue up to 542m/1,779ft, which is incorrectly marked on the ½ inch map as being a wooded top. The terrain is tedious and navigation difficult in this area but the direction is generally eastwards. The route now drops down to the col west of Slieveanard. Here the woods on the north and south are only 100m/yds apart. Slieveanard itself is marked only by a small cairn adjoining a rough forest track. Next the direction is northeast and it is only 60m/200ft uphill to the trig. point at 450m/1,478ft. From here take a bearing to the corner of the woods with a small sheep-pen. A narrow grassy track drops steeply downhill crossing a forest road and ending near a bungalow on the forest edge. The 'seat' at the junction at the top of the 'mountain road', 1.5m/1mile from Cahir, is where your car awaits you.

Distance: 27km/17miles. Ascent: 1,520m/4,900ft. Walking time: 8/10 hours.

At point 613m/2,010ft walkers may wish to head south along the spur west of Kilcoran Lodge Wood and finish on the Cahir-Mitchelstown Road (N8), avoiding the rough ground and least interesting section of the ridge.

Distance: 22km/14miles. Ascent: 1,150m/3,800ft. Time: 7/8½ hours.

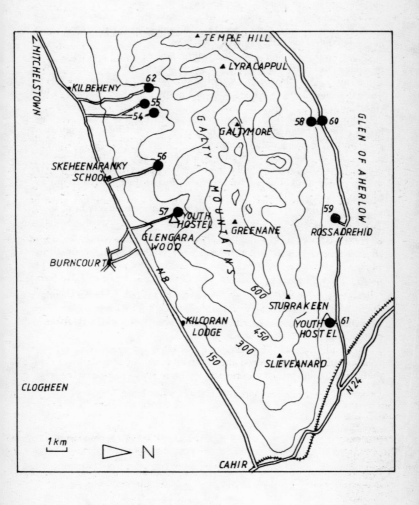

Key map to Galty Mountain walks

63. THE BALLYHOURA MOUNTAINS

The eastern Ballyhouras (Bealach Fheabhrat, Pass of Feabhrat) comprise a relatively narrow plateau distinguished by a number of conglomerate outcrops with interesting and unusual formations.

From the village of Ardpatrick, 642 212, take the R512 south along the road to Fermoy. Turn right after 0.8km/0.5miles, at the first crossroads, and drive uphill for 1km/0.6miles. Park here.

Begin walking uphill along the main forest road and out on to open moorland. Leave the road when you get to the col between 487m/1,600ft and 518m/1,700ft (the road is actually closer to the 1,700ft hill marked on the ½ inch map). Follow a low earth bank at the point where there are tors about 50m/yds.

Follow this line as far as the 518m/1,700ft peak to avoid the thick heather so characteristic of these hills. It is marked by a triangulation point and TV Booster station. Drop down slightly and follow a well-worn path south of east towards Seefin, which at 528m/1,702ft is the highest point of the Ballyhouras. Unlike the other high areas there is no tor here, the summit instead crowned by what is said to be the burial cairn of Finn McCool's poet son Oisin.

Return to the start by retracing your steps (or alternatively head south towards Long Mountain, visiting each of the tors in turn; but walking through the long vegetation can be very tedious).

Distance: 8km/5miles. Ascent: 340m/1,100ft. Walking time: 3 hours.

B. Seefin: Alternative Route

3km/2miles south of Ardpatrick on the L23 take a right turn along a 3rd class road towards the wooded slopes of Seefin (Green Wood). Park after 3km/2miles and take a dirt track on your right which rises gently (with a forest on the left) towards Seefin.

Distance: 3km/2miles. Ascent: 180m/600ft. Walking time: 1½ hours.

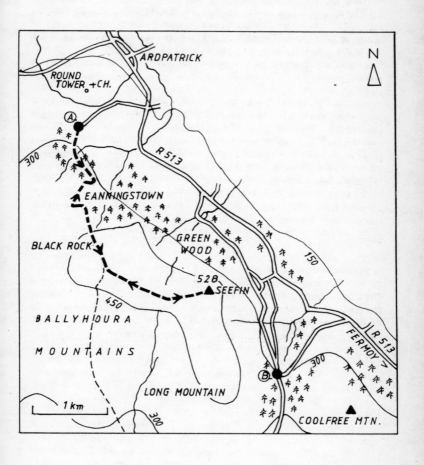

Reference OS Map: Sheet 22 (1:126,720).

↑

This pleasant horseshoe includes crossing the River Mulkeir in two places. It is important to find the best crossing points as it is a substantial river which is too wide and too deep to ford.

Take the R499 west from Silvermines village and after about 4km/ 2.5miles you will come to a junction where you take the road running south. After 3km/2miles turn in to the river valley between the Silvermines ridge to the north and Keeper Hill to the south. Park about 1.5km/ 1mile along it, close to a farm surrounded by trees on the left, 791 689. (This road continues right through the valley, though only a section of it is marked on the ½ inch OS map.)

Cross the fields by the farm and head uphill in a north-easterly direction until you reach the top of the ridge at about 360m/1,200ft. Then turn right and follow the edge of low crags. From here it is very easy walking in a mixture of rock and boggy terrain to the little cairn at 462m/1,515ft. The highest point of the ridge is reached further along.

There are fine views south across the valley to Keeper Hill. Below you on the left are the ugly waste heaps of the mines for which the mountain is named. Lead, zinc and silver were first found in this area in the fourteenth century but mining is not carried on any longer.

Soon after 490m/1,609ft, you drop down to a col which leads to the first of the forests which almost cover the eastern end of the ridge. A stream flows southwards (not marked on ½ inch OS map) by the edge of the forest. Before reaching the trees turn right and head down the southern side of the hill towards the road in the valley. Cross the road by the bridge and turn right towards a lane leading to a farm on the bank of the Mulkeir River. The lane goes through the farmyard. Just behind the farmyard, turn left towards the river where you will find a timber footbridge spanning what is otherwise a difficult stream to cross.

Now start uphill again, southwards along a dirt track and through fields towards Keeper Hill. Stay to the right of a forest not marked on ½ inch OS map. This is a tedious ascent of nearly 400m/1,300ft over thick heather and long grassy vegetation, and you will be relieved to reach the summit cairn 694m/2,279ft. The view from the summit is rewarding with the Silvermines ridge to the north and numerous low hills, often wooded, dominating the landscape in all directions. It was on the west side of Keeper Hill in 1690 that Patrick Sarsfield and his men camped before successfully ambushing the Williamite siege train at Ballyneety, Co. Limerick.

From the summit cairn, head slightly downhill towards the northwest corner of the plateau where two small stone piles overlook a roughly circular bed of boulders probably prehistoric in origin. Just beyond them is the attractive little corrie of Eagles Nest. The corrie itself does not contain a lake and is forested. Above the forest there are a number of crags not marked on the ½ inch OS map, which could be dangerous in misty conditions.

Now make your way round the rim of the corries and then towards a large forest. Drop down to the corner of the forest and a dirt track (this track is used by cattle and could be very muddy in winter). Turn left and walk along the track until you come to derelict farm buildings. Cross two fields by the farm, keeping to the left until you come to a gate leading to a green road. Follow this road down to the rough track which continues down to the river, cross here by a bridge and you will then emerge close to where you parked your car.

Distance: 11km/7miles. Ascent: 890m/2,900ft. Walking time: 5 hours.

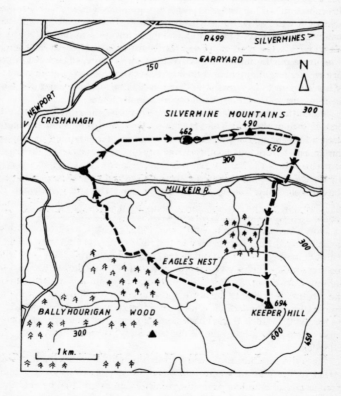

Reference OS Map: Sheet 18 (1:126,720).

65. THE DEVIL'S BIT

The Devil's Bit is a curious notch clearly visible over a wide area. The Devil is reputed to have bitten a large piece from the ridge of the Devil's Bit Mountain and finding it distasteful spat it out. It landed 20 miles south, in the Golden Vale at Cashel where it forms the 'Rock of Cashel'. However, it must have undergone a major metamorphosis, as the Rock of Cashel is limestone and the mountain of origin is composed of Silurian grits. Geologists believe the gorge known as the Gap was the result of breaching during glacial times.

From Templemore take the road southwest towards Borrisoleigh. When you come to a junction after 5km/3miles, take the right turn. After about 2km/1.25miles you will encounter another junction — Golding's Cross. Go straight ahead to the top of the road at the col — 044 740 — between 463m/1,521ft and the Devil's Bit mountain, where there is ample parking. A word of warning! The army use this area as a firing range so keep clear when the red flag is flying at the gateway on the left.

Follow a wide road north-eastwards towards the forest. The large white cross on the top of the steep-sided tor will soon become visible. Turn right along the road and then turn left and follow the spur along a well-worn path to the cross. The Cross itself, 13m/45ft high and made of concrete, was erected in 1953 and is permanently lit up.

Descend by the same path and turn left under the cliffs to reach the gorge known as the Gap. This is the 'Bite'. Cross the 'Bite' along a path to where a short scramble will take you to the top of a bare plateau of grey silurian rocks and low heather to a triangulation station marking the summit at 478m/1,577ft. The plateau is bounded on all sides by low cliffs so care should be taken when descending. Therefore, it is prudent to follow the same line back to the Gap and retrace your steps to the road.

Distance: 5km/3miles. Ascent: 240m/800ft. Walking time: 2 hours.

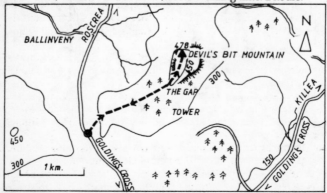

Reference OS Map: Sheet 18 (1:126,720).

66. GLENBARROW CIRCUIT

From the village of Rosenallis take the road for Mountrath and 1.2km/
0.75miles from Rosenallis at a T-junction turn right (northwest).

Take note that many signposts are brown and white. These are direction signposts to amenity areas.

Follow the direction signpost indicating 'Glenbarrow Valley Forest Walk' and 2km/1.25miles along this straight road, at a small crossroads, turn southwest into Glenbarrow.

1.5km/1mile along this winding lane you arrive at Glenbarrow carpark, 368 082, the start of this walk and also the start of the long-distance walk 'The Slieve Bloom Way'.

From the carpark take the lane signposted to the Ridge of Caspard. Continue along the forest road and 1.5km/1mile farther on, at the forest boundary, turn left southeast and continue uphill to the ridge.

Leaving the metal pylons of the telecommunications relay station behind you on your left, follow the markers of the Slieve Bloom Way, taking the rough track southwest for 50m/yds to the tarmac road.

From the tarmac road continue southwest across the heather along the ridge, crossing a track which leads to the forest plantation visible on your right. Do not be tempted to continue on this track until nearer the plantation as the ascent to the ridge from that point is through sodden marsh and deep heather. Keep high on the ridge where the shorter heather gradually gives way to the bedrock of the mountain range.

In the distance, weather permitting, the large stone cairn known locally as the Stoney Man will be visible, 347 048. This cairn is often mistaken for the summit of Clarnahinch Mountain (483m/1,585ft) but is in fact a cairn on the spoil heap of a small, long-abandoned sandstone quarry. The hollows at the cairn are an excellent spot to shelter from the driving rain or chilling wind or to have lunch and appreciate the views as far northeast, east, and southwest as the eye can see. In ideal conditions the mountains of Wicklow, the Blackstairs, Comeraghs, Silvermines and Galtees can be seen.

At this point you leave the Slieve Bloom Way to continue southwest from the cairn over the heather-clad unmarked summit of Clarnahinch Mountain to the col beyond.

Baunreaghcong (509m/1,670ft) with its small heathery cairn rises from the far side of the col. The easiest line of ascent is alongside the deep furrow ploughed before the upland blanket bog became a National Nature Reserve.

From Baunreaghcong continue west-northwest for almost 2km/1.25miles to Barna (504m/1,654ft). When plodding through the energy-sapping heather, the hillwalkers' rest (to stop for the view or the photograph!) is richly rewarded with the complete panorama of Glenbarrow and views across the Bog of Allen far to the north.

From the summit of Barna, marked by a heather-covered cairn, descend north-northeast to the source of the River Barrow, and continuing in the same direction you will shortly rejoin the Slieve Bloom Way. Head first in a northeast direction and then eastwards overlooking the Glenlahan Valley on your left.

As you walk along, you will see the stumps of the ancient pine forest which covered this area some six thousand years ago, now uprooted and exposed in the course of modern forest planting. Some stumps still cling to their leathery bark long preserved in the bog.

When the pylons on the opposite side of the valley become visible, keep a watch for the Slieve Bloom Way marker on the left of the road; its yellow arrow indicates the easiest way to descend to the river below.

Cross the river by way of the timber footbridge 360 069 and continue on the east bank of the river, past the waterfall, the cliffs of glacial till and along the forest path to the carpark.

Distance: 16km/10miles. Ascent: 440m/1,450ft. Walking time: 5½ hours.

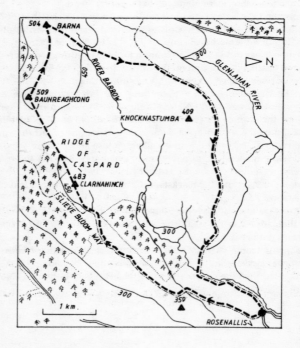

Reference OS Map: Sheet 54 (1:50,000).

67. GLENLETTER CIRCUIT

From Cadamstown take the R421 southwest towards Kinnitty for 2km/ 1.25miles. At Lackaroe Crossroads turn left (signposted Glenletter) and continue for 5km/3miles to the car park at the forest entrance 100m/yds beyond Letter Crossroads 254 044.

From the carpark walk south of east uphill on the tarred road for 1.5km/1mile. Take the gravel road to the left passing the triangulation point for Wolftrap Mountain (487m/1,598ft) on your right and continue on this gravel road to its end among the forest communications masts and stay wires.

At the end of the road continue due north across the heather to the edge of the forest plantation. The panoramic views to the north and west are spectacular. At the edge of the forest you could find a deer track which will greatly ease your passage through the heather northwest towards the unmarked summit of Spink (330m/1,100ft).

On your way you will pass some small turf banks still in use and others abandoned to the encroaching heather. These turf banks are shallow, being, as is said, only two boards deep — a board being the depth of turf sod cut by the slean. Continue from the turf banks by the bog road which leads to a forest road.

At the forest road 253 071 turn left, southwest. From this point you are on the route of the Slieve Bloom Way and the markers with their yellow arrows will be an aid to your route finding. 100m/yds farther on, cross the stile to the left of the wooden gate and continue on the forest road through the plantation to the river valley below.

Cross the Silver River at the ford, continue up the road and turn left (due south) at the small junction 253 074.

Approximately 1km/0.6miles along this rough road, at the edge of the river, enter the forest plantation by the wooden gate on the right, 236 067.

This small path was in times past a laneway to a now long abandoned cottage which you will pass farther on.

The walk continues along a wide forest cutting which will no doubt become a forest road in the future. Where the cutting eventually meets the plantation road proper, turn left due west and continue to the tarred country road above.

At this tarred road 229 057 turn due south and you will have fine views of Glenletter and Barlahan (*Barr*, summit/top; *lahan*, broad) as you make your way along this road to Letter Crossroads and the car park.

Distance: 13km/9miles. Ascent: 300m/2,000ft. Walking time: 4 hours.

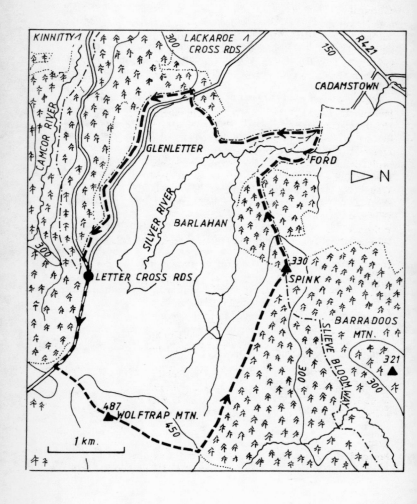

Reference OS Map: Sheet 54 (1:50,000).

BIBLIOGRAPHY

General

Charlesworth, J.K., *The Geology of Ireland — An Introduction*, London 1966.

Fairley, J., *An Irish Beast Book* (revised ed.), Belfast 1984.

Gillmor, D. (ed.), *The Irish Countryside*, Dublin 1989.

Graves, R., *The White Goddess (A Tree Alphabet)*, London 1961.

Harbison, P., *Guide to the National Monuments of Ireland* (2nd ed.), Dublin 1975.

Harbison, P. (ed.), *The Shell Guide to Ireland*, Dublin 1989.

Holland, C.H. (ed.), *A Geology of Ireland*, Edinburgh 1981.

Hutchinson, E.D., *Birds in Ireland*, Calton 1989.

Joyce, P.W., *Irish Names of Places* (3 vols), London 1973.

Lynam, J., *Irish Peaks*, London 1982.

Mulholland, H., *Guide to Ireland's 3000-foot Mountains*, Wirral 1988.

Praeger, Robert L., *The Way that I Went*, Dublin 1969.

Wall, C.W., *Mountaineering in Ireland*, Dublin 1976.

Webb, D.A., *An Irish Flora*, Dundalk 1977.

Wilson & Gilbert, *Classic Walks*, London 1982.

Wilson & Gilbert, *Wild Walks*, London 1988.

Whittow, J.B., *Geology and Scenery in Ireland*, Harmondsworth 1974.

East

Brunker, J.P., *The Flora of County Wicklow*, Dundalk 1950.

Fewer, M., *The Wicklow Way*, Dublin 1988.

Herman, D., *Hill Walkers Wicklow*, 1989.

Herman, D., *Hill Strollers Wicklow*, 1990.

Hutchinson, C., *Birds of Dublin and Wicklow*, Dublin 1975.

Irish Ramblers Club, *Dublin and Wicklow Mountains — Access Routes for the Hill Walker*, 1988.

Joyce, W. St J., *The Neighbourhood of Dublin*, Dublin 1971.

Malone, J.B., *The Complete Wicklow Way*, Dublin 1988.

Moriarty, C., *On Foot in Dublin and Wicklow*, Dublin 1989.

Price, L., *The Place Names of County Wicklow* (7 vols.), Dublin 1967.

South

Power, P.C., *Heritage Trails in South Tipperary*, Clonmel 1987.

Warner, P., *A Visitor's Guide to the Comeragh Mountains*, Belfast 1978.

GLOSSARY

Glossary of the more common Irish words used in Place Names

Abha, abhainn (ow, owen)   river
Achadh (agha, augh)   field
Ail or *Faill*   cliff
Alt   height or side of glen
Ard   height, promontory
Ath   ford

Baile (bally)   town, townland
Bán (bawn, baun)   white
Barr   top
Beag (beg)   small
Bealach (ballagh)   pass
Beann (ben)   peak or pointed mountain
Bearna (barna)   gap
Bignian   little peak
Bó   cow
Bóthar (boher)   road
Bothairin (bohereen)   small (unsurfaced) road
Breac (brack)   speckled
Brí (bree, bray)   hill
Buaile (booley)   summer dairy pasture
Buí   yellow
Bun   foot of anything, river mouth

Carn   pile of stones
Carraig (carrick)   a rock
Cathair (caher)   stone fort
Ceann (ken)   head, headland
Ceathramhadh (carrow)   quarter of land
Ceapach   plot of tillage ground
Cill   cell, church
Clár   plain, board
Cloch   stone
Clochóg   stepping stones
Cluain (cloon)   meadow
Cnoc (knock, crock)   hill
Coill (kyle, kill)   wood
Coire   cauldron, corrie
Cor   rounded hill
Corrán (carraun)   sickle, serrated mountain
Cruach, cruachan   steep hill (rick)
Cúm (coum)   hollow, corrie

168

Dearg   red
Doire (derry)   oakgrove
Druim   ridge
Dubh (duff, doo)   black
Dún   fort, castle

Eas (ass)   waterfall
Eisc (esk)   steep, rocky gully

Fionn (fin)   white, clear
Fraoch (freagh)   heath, heather

Gabhar (gower)   goat
Gaoith (gwee)   wind
Glas   green
Glais   streamlet
Gleann (glen)   valley
Gort   tilled field

Inbhear (inver)   river mouth
Inis   island

Lágh (law)   hill
Leac   flagstone
Leaca, leacan (lackan)   side of a hill
Leacht   huge heap of stones
Learg   side of a hill
Leitir (letter)   wet hillside
Liath (lea)   grey
Loch (lough)   lake or sea inlet
Lug, lag   hollow

Machaire (maghera)   plain
Mael, maol (mweel)   bald, bare hill
Maigh   plain
Mám, madhm (maum)   pass
Más   long, low hill
Mór (more)   big
Muing   long-grassed expanse
Mullach   summit

Oilean   island

Poll   hole, pond

Riabhach   grey
Rinn   headland
Rua, ruadh   red

Scairbh (scarriff)   shallow ford
Scealp   rocky cleft
Sceilig (skellig)   rock
Sceir (sker, pl. skerry)   rock, reef (Norse)
Sean   old
Sescenn (seskin)   marsh
Sidh (shee)   fairy, fairy hill
Sliabh (slieve)   mountain
Slidhe (slee)   road, track
Spinc   pointed pinnacle
Srón   nose, noselike mountain feature
Sruth, sruthair, sruthán   stream
Stuaic (stook)   pointed pinnacle
Súi, suidhe (see)   seat

Taobh, taebh (tave)   side, hillside
Teach   house
Teampull   church
Tír (teer)   land, territory
Tobar   well
Tor   tower-like rock
Torc   wild boar
Tulach   little hill